Yonder

Siri Hustvedt

Yonder

Essays

HENRY HOLT AND COMPANY   NEW YORK

Henry Holt and Company, Inc.
Publishers since 1866
115 West 18th Street
New York, New York 10011

Henry Holt® is a registered trademark of
Henry Holt and Company, Inc.

Library of Congress Cataloging-in-Publication Data
Hustvedt, Siri.
Yonder: essays / Siri Hustvedt.—1st ed.
p.   cm.
ISBN 0-8050-5011-6 (hardbound: alk. paper)
I. Title.
PS3558.U813Y66   1998   97-28891
814'.54—dc21   CIP

Henry Holt books are available for special promotions and premiums.
For details contact: Director, Special Markets.

First Edition 1998

Designed by Kelly Soong

Printed in the United States of America
All first editions are printed on acid-free paper. ∞
1   3   5   7   9   10   8   6   4   2

Essays in this collection have previously appeared in
Brick, Conjunctions, and *Modern Painters.*

For Ester Vegan Hustvedt and Lloyd Hustvedt

Contents

Yonder

Yonder

1

My father once asked me if I knew where yonder was. I said I thought *yonder* was another word for *there*. He smiled and said, "No, yonder is between here and there." This little story has stayed with me for years as an example of linguistic magic: it identified a new space—a middle region that was neither here nor there—a place that simply didn't exist for me until it was given a name. During my father's brief explanation of the meaning of *yonder*, and every time I've thought of it since, a landscape appears in my mind: I am standing at the crest of a small hill looking down into an open valley where there is a single tree, and beyond it lies the horizon defined by a series of low mountains or hills. This dull but serviceable image returns every time I think of *yonder*, one of those wonderful words I later discovered linguists call "shifters"—words distinct from others because they are animated by the speaker and move accordingly. In linguistic terms this means that you can never really find yourself *yonder*. Once you arrive at yonder tree, it becomes *here* and recedes forever into that imaginary horizon. Words that wobble attract me. The fact that *here* and *there* slide and slip depending on where I am is somehow poignant to me, revealing both the tenuous relation between words and things and the miraculous flexibility of language.

The truth is that what fascinates me is not so much being in a place as *not* being there: how places live in the mind once you have left them, how they are imagined before you arrive, or how they are seemingly called out of nothing to illustrate a thought or story like my tree down yonder. These mental spaces map our inner lives more fully than any "real" map, delineating the borders of *here* and *there* that also shape what we see in the present. My private geography, like most peoples', excludes huge portions of the world. I have my own version of the famous Saul Steinberg map of the United States that shows a towering Manhattan; a shrunken, nearly invisible Midwest, South, and West; and ends in a more prominent California featuring Los Angeles. There have been only three important places in my life: Northfield, Minnesota, where I was born and grew up with my parents and three younger sisters; Norway, birthplace of my mother and my father's grandparents; and New York City, where I have now lived for the past seventeen years.

When I was a child, the map consisted of two regions only: Minnesota and Norway, my here and my there. And although each remained distinct from the other—Norway was far away across the ocean and Minnesota was immediate, visible, and articulated into the thousands of subdivisions that make up everyday geography—the two places intermingled in language. I spoke Norwegian before I spoke English. Literally my mother's tongue, Norwegian remains for me a language of childhood, of affection, of food, and of songs. I often feel its rhythms beneath my English thoughts and prose, and sometimes its vocabulary invades both. I spoke Norwegian first, because my maternal grandmother came to stay in Northfield before I had my first birthday and lived with us for nine months; but after she returned home, I began learning English and forgot Norwegian. It came back to me when I traveled with my mother and sister to Norway in 1959. During those months in Norway, when I was four years old and my sister Liv was only two and a half, we forgot English. When we found ourselves back in Minnesota, we remembered English and promptly forgot Norwegian again. Although the language went dormant for us, it lived on in our house. My parents often spoke Norwegian to each other, and there were words Liv and I and Astrid and Ingrid used habitually and supposed were English words but were not. For example, the Norwegian words for *bib*, *sausage*, *peeing*, and *butt* all submerged their English equivalents. Liv and I remember using these words with friends and how surprised we were to see their befuddled faces. The paraphernalia of infancy, of food, and inevitably the language of the toilet were so connected to our mother that they existed only in Norwegian. When I was twelve, my father, a professor of Norwegian language and literature, took a sabbatical year in Bergen, and Norwegian came back to me in a kind of flash. After that, it stuck. The speed with which we four sisters transferred our lives into Norwegian is nothing short of remarkable. During that year we played, thought, and dreamed in Norwegian.

I returned to Norway in 1972 and attended gymnasium in Bergen for a year. That time my family was not with me. I lived with my aunt and uncle outside the city and took the bus to school. Sometime during the initial weeks of my stay, I had a dream. I cannot remember its content, but the dream took place in Norwegian with English subtitles. I will always think of that dream as limbo. Its cinematic code expressed precisely my place between two cultures and two languages. But soon the metaphorical subtitles of my life disappeared, and I immersed myself in the dream's "original" language. It has now been twenty-three years since I really *lived* in Norwegian. It surprises even me that less than three of my forty years were actually spent in Norway and that nearly every minute of that time was lived in Bergen. I speak Norwegian with such a broad Bergen dialect that my parents find it comical. That dialect is the real legacy of my years in Bergen, the imprint of an experience that will not leave me. Chances are even senility won't rob me of it, since the old and feebleminded often return to the language of early childhood. And yet Norwegian survives in me not only as a sign of Bergen but as a sign of my parents' house in Minnesota. It is not for nothing, after all, that when my stepson, Daniel, was a very little boy and he looked forward to going home to Minnesota with me and his father for Christmas, he would ask, "When are we going to Norway?"

If language is the most profound feature of any place, and I think it is, then perhaps my childhood history of forgetting and remembering enacts in miniature the dialectic of all immigrant experience: *here* and *there* are in a relation of constant strain that is chiefly determined by memory. My father, who is a third-generation Norwegian, speaks English with a Norwegian accent, testament to an American childhood that was lived largely in Norwegian. Although separated by an ocean, my mother and father grew up speaking the same language.

My mother was thirty years old when she came to the United States to live for good. She is now an American citizen and claims she is glad of this every time she votes. My mother's threat to take the first plane back to Norway if Goldwater was elected remains strong in my memory, however. Norway was always there, and it

was always calling. A Fulbright scholarship brought my father to
the University of Oslo, where he met my mother. The details of
how the two met are unknown to me. What is mythologized in
some families was private in ours. My mother's sister once used
the English expression "love at first sight" to describe that
encounter, but I have never felt any reason to poke my nose into
what is clearly their business. Oslo may not be Paris, but it's a lot
bigger than Northfield and a lot less provincial, and when my
mother traveled from one place to the other to marry my father,
whose family she had never laid eyes on, she must have imagined
the place that lay ahead. She must have seen in her mind a world
my father had described at least in part to her, but whether that
world tallied with what she actually found is another question
altogether. What is certain is that she left a world behind her. As a
child she lived in Mandal, the most southern city in Norway, and
those years were by every account (not only my mother's) idyllic.
Her memories from the first ten years of her life, with her parents,
two brothers, and a sister in a beautiful house above the city
where her father was postmaster, are ones of such aching happiness that she says she sometimes kept her memories from me and
my three sisters in fear that we might feel deprived in comparison.
When she was ten years old, her father lost his money and his
land. He had undersigned a business deal for a relative that went
sour. Although he might have saved himself from ruin, my grandfather kept his word of honor and paid on that debt, which wasn't
really his, for the rest of his life. I think this event forms the great-
est divide in my mother's life. Suddenly and irrevocably, it cut
her off from the home she loved and threw her into another as
surely as if the earth had opened up and formed an impassable
chasm between the two. The family moved to Askim, outside of
Oslo, and this is why my mother's voice carries traces of both a

southern accent and an eastern one: the mingled sounds from either side of the chasm. I have never doubted the happiness of my mother's first ten years, in Mandal. She had parents who loved her, rocks and mountains and ocean just beyond her doorstep. There were maids to lighten housework, siblings and family close by, and Christmases celebrated hard and long at home and in the house of tante Andora and onkel Andreas, people I have imagined repeatedly but seen only in photographs taken when they were too young to have been the aunt and uncle my mother knew. But it seems to me that losing paradise makes it all the more radiant, not only for my mother but, strangely enough, for me. It is an odd but emotionally resonant coincidence that every time I have been in Mandal, it doesn't rain. Rain is the torment of all Norwegians, who seek the sun with a fervor that might look a little desperate to, say, a person from California. The truth is it rains a lot in Norway. But when my mother took us there in 1959, it was a summer of legendary sunshine, and when I was last in Mandal, for a family reunion in 1991 with my mother and sisters and my own daughter, the sun shone for days on end, and the city gleamed in the clear, perfect light of heaven.

I never knew my grandfather. He died when my mother was nineteen. There are photographs of him, one in which he stands facing a white horse with three young children on its back. He is wearing a straw hat that shades his eyes, and between his lips is a cigarette. What is most striking in the picture is his posture, proud and erect, but with another quality that is almost but not quite jaunty. It is somehow obvious that he didn't strike a pose. He had intelligent features—his eyes especially give the impression of thought. My grandmother said he read (almost to the exclusion of anything else) church history and Kierkegaard. She adored him and never married again. I'm sure it never entered her

mind to do so. When I think of my mother's mother, I think of
her voice, her gestures, and her touch. They were all soft, all
refined; and, at the same time, she was freely and passionately
affectionate. For some reason, I remember with tremendous clarity
walking through her door, when I was twelve, with my sisters and
my mother and father. It was winter and my mother had knit me a
new white hat and scarf to go with my brown coat. When my
grandmother greeted me, she put her hands on either side of my
face and said, "You're so beautiful in white, my darling."

The last time I lived in Norway, I visited my grandmother
every day after school. She lived in a tiny apartment that rose
above a small, old graveyard in the city. She was always happy to
see me. I'm afraid I was a morbidly serious adolescent that year, a
girl who read Faulkner and Baldwin, Keats and Marx with equal
reverence, and I must have been somewhat humorless company.
But there was no one I liked being with more than her, and this
may have made me livelier. We drank coffee. We talked. She loved
Dickens, whom she read in Norwegian. Years after she was dead, I
wrote a dissertation on Charles Dickens, and though my study of
the great man would no doubt have alarmed her, I had a funny
feeling that by taking on the English novelist, I was returning to
my Norwegian roots.

My *mormor* (in Norwegian maternal and paternal lines are
distinguished: *mormor* literally means "mother-mother") is at the
center of my real experiences of Norway, Norway as particular and
daily, as one home. She was a *lady* in the old sense of the word,
the word that corresponds to *gentleman*—a person who never
shed her nineteenth-century heritage of gentility. I was deep in my
self-righteous socialist phase, and I'll never forget her saying to me
in her soft voice, "You must be the first person in the family to
march in a May Day parade." She wore a hat and gloves every time

she went out, dusted her impeccable apartment daily, including each and every picture frame that hung on the wall, and was shocked when her cleaning lady used the familiar form *du* when she spoke to her. I can recall her small apartment very well—the elegant blue sofa—the pictures on the wall—the shining table— the birdcage that held her parakeet Bitte Liten, a name I would translate as "the tiny one." And I remember every object with fierce affection. Had I not loved my grandmother, and had she not loved my mother very well and loved me, those things would just be things. After Mormor died, I walked with my own mother outside our house in Minnesota, and she said to me that the strangest part of her mother's death was that a person who had only wanted the best for her wasn't there anymore. I recall exactly where the two of us were standing in the yard when she said it. I remember the summer weather, the slight browning of the grass from the heat, the woods at our left. It's as if I inscribed her words into that particular landscape, and the funny thing is that they are still written there for me. Not long after that conversation, I dreamed that my grandmother was alive and spoke to me. I don't remember what she said in the dream, but it was one of those dreams in which you are conscious that the person is dead but is suddenly alive and with you again. Although all other architectural detail is lost, I know I was sitting in a room and my grandmother walked through a door toward me. It was a threshold dream, a spatial reversal of my memory of walking through her door and her telling me I was beautiful in white. I remember how intensely happy I was to see her.

My daughter, Sophie, has always called my mother "Mormor," and no name could be more evocative of the maternal line. Mother-mother is for me an incantation of pregnancy and birth itself, of one person coming from another, and then its repetition in time. When I was pregnant with Sophie, I felt it was the only time I had been physically plural—two in one. But of course it had happened before, when I was the one inside that first place. Uterine space is mysterious. We can't remember its liquid reality, but we know now that the fetus hears voices. After the violence of birth (all the classes, breathing, and birth-cult nonsense in the world do not make the event nonviolent), the newborn's recognition of his or her mother's voice forms a bridge across that first, brutal separation.

2

By its very nature, original space, maternal space, is nonsense; human experience there is undifferentiated and so can't be put into words. It lives on in our bodies, however, when we curl up to sleep, when we eat, when some of us bathe or swim. And surely it leaves its traces in our physical desire for another. Paternal space in an ideal sense is different. Although we are "of" our fathers, just as we are "of" our mothers, we were never "in" our fathers. Their separateness is obvious. In the real lives of real people, this distance may be exaggerated or diminished. A lot of children of my generation grew up with more or less absent fathers. I didn't. My father was very much *there* in my life and in the lives of my sisters, and like my mother, he was fundamentally shaped by the place where he grew up.

He was born in a log house in 1922, not far from Cannon Falls, Minnesota. That house burned and the family moved close by, to the house where my grandparents lived throughout my childhood. That house never had plumbing, but there was a pump in the front yard. My sisters and I loved that rusty pump. I remember being so small I had to reach for the handle and then, using both hands and all my weight, I would pull down several times and wait for the gush of water. My father remembers a world of barn raisings, quilting bees, traveling peddlers, square dances, and sleighs pulled by horses. He attended a one-room schoolhouse, all grades together, and he was confirmed in Norwegian at Urland Church—a white wooden church with a steeple that stands at the top of a hill. For me, that church is a sign of proximity. When we reached the church in the family car, it meant we could spot my grandparents' house. The church was the last landmark in a series of landmarks, to which my sisters and I gave such inventive names as "the big hill." Every landmark was accompanied by an equally inventive song: "We are going down the big hill. We are going down the big hill." My parents were subjected to this for years. The trip was about seventeen miles and took about half an hour on the small roads. My sisters and I, like most children, were creatures of repetition and ritual. Places revisited were given a sacred and enchanted quality. I use those words carefully, because there was something liturgical about going over the same ground so many times. The products of both Lutheran Sunday school and fairy tales, we infused the places where we grew up with what we knew best.

Despite the fact that my parents shared a language, the worlds in which each of them grew up were very different. The Norwegian American immigrant communities formed in the Midwest in the nineteenth century and the country left behind were separated not only by miles but by culture. Those "little Norways" developed very differently from the motherland, even linguistically. The dialects people brought with them took another course on the prairie. English words with no Norwegian equivalents were brought into spoken Norwegian and given gender. Norwegians who visited relations who had lived in America for several generations were surprised by their antiquated diction and grammar. The legacy of homesteading, of primitive life on the prairie, along with the real distance from the country of origin, kept the nineteenth century alive longer in America than in many parts of Norway.

My grandparents' small farm, reduced to twenty acres in my lifetime, was our playground, but even as a child I sensed the weight of the past, not only on that property, which was no longer farmed, but in the community as a whole. I lived to see it vanish. The old people are dead. Many of the little farms have been sold and bought up by agribusinesses, and when you walk into a store or visit a neighbor, people don't speak Norwegian anymore. When my grandmother died, at ninety-eight, my father spoke at her funeral. He called her "the last pioneer." My father shuns all forms of cliché and false sentiment. He meant it. She was among the very last of the people who remembered life on the prairie. My paternal grandmother, a feisty, outspoken, not entirely rational woman, especially when it came to politics, banks, and social issues, could tell a good story. She had a swift and lean approach to narrative that nevertheless included the apt, particular detail. I often wish now I had recorded these stories on tape. When she was six years old, Matilda Underdahl lost her mother. The story, which became myth in our family, is this: When the local pastor told Tilly her mother's death was "God's will," she stamped her foot and screamed, "No, it's not!" My grandmother retained a suspicion of religious pieties all her life. She remembered the polio epidemic that killed many people she knew, and in a brief but vivid story, she made it real for me. She was sitting with her father at a window, watching two coffins being carried out of a neighboring house—one large and one small. As they watched, her father spoke to her in a low voice. "We must pray," he said, "and eat onions." She remembered a total eclipse of the sun, and she said she was told that the world was going to end. They dressed themselves in their Sunday clothes, sat down in the house, folded their hands, and waited. She remembered being told about the *nokken* in the well, a water monster that pulled little children down to the depths where it lived and probably ate them. Clearly meant to scare children from getting too close to the well and drowning, the story lured little Matilda straight to it. And there she tempted fate. She laid her head on the well's edge and let her long red curls dangle far down inside as she waited in stubborn, silent horror for the *nokken* to come.

But there is another small story I heard only once that has lasted in my mind. When she was a child, she lived near a lake in Minnesota in Ottertail County; and during the winter, when that lake froze, she and the other children would take their sleds onto the lake and fit them out with sails. I can't remember what they used for sails, but when the wind was up, the sails would fill with air and propel the sleds across the ice, sometimes at great speed. When she told me this, her voice communicated her pleasure in this memory, and I saw those sleds from a distance, three or four on the wide expanse of a frozen lake gliding noiselessly across it. That is how I still imagine it. I don't see or hear the children. What she remembered is undoubtedly something so radically different from the image I gave to her memory that the two may be incompatible. My great-grandfather on my mother's side was a sea captain. There is a painting of his ship that my uncle has now. She was called *Mars*. It may be that I have linked that painting of a great sailing ship on the ocean with the tiny ships on the ice in landlocked Minnesota, but I'm not sure. Tilly's family came from Underdahl in the Sogn Fjord. She never went there, but I saw Underdahl with my parents and sisters as we traveled by boat down the fjord where the mountainsides are so steep that farmers have traditionally used ladders to descend into the towns below. Underdahl has a tiny church. From the boat, the white structure looked almost doll-like, and the name for me has come to mean not only my grandmother but that miniature building.

The Depression hit my paternal grandparents hard. They weren't alone, of course, but my father's life was and is shaped by that hardship—of this I am certain. He has many stories about the people he grew up with, but his inner life and the pictures he carries with him, in particular the most painful ones, are hidden to me. I know that my father began working on other farms when he was ten years old. I know that my grandmother made and sold *lefse*, a flat potato cake, to bring in money. I know that there was a 1,200-dollar debt on the farm that couldn't be paid once the Depression hit. Forty acres of the sixty-acre farm were lost. I know that after the United States entered the war, my grandfather, like so many others, found work in a local defense plant. He was transferred to a town in Washington State and had to leave the family. He worked building the defense plant where the atomic bomb would later be manufactured. But he didn't know this until years later. Many people in that community worked themselves sick and silly, and their labor didn't prevent catastrophes of weather or economy, and people died of them—physically and spiritually. It has become a truism to say that there was much that was unforgiving and brutal about that life, but it is nevertheless a fact, and by the time I saw the world where my father had lived as a child, a kind of stasis had set in. I remember how still my grandparents' farm was. The enormous sky and the flat fields and the absence of traffic on the road that ran past that place were only part of it. There was an inner stillness, too.

High in the mountains above the town of Voss, in western Norway, lies the farm that gave me my name: Hustveit. At some point, the *tveit* became *tvedt*, a different spelling for the same word, which means an opening or a clearing. I have been there. The place is now owned and cared for by the Norwegian government. You have to climb a mountain to reach Hustveit, and a landscape more different from the Minnesota prairie could hardly be imagined. I wondered what my great-grandfather saw when he imagined "Amerika." Could he have seen in his mind a landscape as open and flat as what he actually came to? Immigration inevitably involves error and revision. What I imagined it would be, it's not. For better or worse, some mistake is unavoidable.

My sisters and I loved to listen to a simple story about an immigrant's mistake in our own family. My grandfather's first cousin, whom my sisters and I called Uncle David, left Hustveit when he was twenty-two years old to make his way in America alone. He arrived at Ellis Island in August 1902. He spent his first day in New York City and was flabbergasted by the chaos, color, and crowds. Somewhere in the city, he saw a man selling apples, the most gorgeous, red, perfect apples he had ever seen. He had almost no money, but he lusted after one of those apples, and, overcome by desire, he splurged and bought one. The story goes that he lifted the apple to his mouth, bit into it, and spat it out in disgust. It was a tomato. Uncle David had never seen or heard of a tomato. My sisters and I roared with laughter at this story. It encapsulates so neatly the lesson of expectation and reality that it could serve as a parable. The fact that tomatoes are good is beside the point. If you think you're getting an apple, a tomato will revolt you. That New York should be nicknamed the Big Apple, that an apple is the fruit of humankind's first error and the expulsion from paradise, that America and paradise have been linked and confused ever since Europeans first hit its shores, makes the story reverberate as myth.

On the other hand, if not violently overthrown, expectation can have a power in itself, can invest a place with what literally isn't there. When I saw Hustveit, I felt the same reverence I felt the last time I was in Mandal. They are both beautiful places, it is true, the stuff of postcards and nineteenth-century landscape painting, but no doubt I would have felt reverent in less lovely places, because I imagined a past I connected to myself. Walking beside my mother up toward the house where she lived with her parents and siblings, I imagined what she must have felt walking over that ground where she walked as a child, remembering people now dead, especially her father and her mother, and that empathy provoked in me deep feeling. My father never lived at Hustveit, nor did his father, but it was a strong presence in both their lives. In 1961, out of the blue, my grandfather Lars Hustvedt inherited 5,850 crowns, about 850 dollars, from a Norwegian relative, Anna Hustveit. He used the money to travel to Norway for the first and last time, visiting Voss and Hustveit during the trip. He was seventy-four years old. My grandfather's sojourn in Norway was a great success. According to my father, he impressed his relatives with his intimate knowledge of Hustveit. He knew exactly where every building on the property lay and what it looked like from his father, who had described his birthplace in detail to his son. Hustveit was and is a real place, but it is also a sign of origin. I don't doubt that there were times when that sign alone, carried from one generation to another in a name, accompanied by a mental image, anchored the people who had left it and anchored their children and grandchildren as well in another place, crushed by the vicissitudes of nature and politics.

My grandfather remembered what he had never seen. He remembered it through someone else. It is no doubt a tribute to his character and to his father's that the image handed down from one to the other seems to have been remarkably accurate. Every story is given some kind of mental ground. The expression "I see" in English for "I understand" is hardly haphazard. We are always providing pictures for what we hear. My mother and father both lived through World War II, my mother in occupied Norway and my father as a soldier in New Guinea, the Philippines, and finally in Japan during the occupation. They were both inside that immense historical cataclysm. Each has a story of how it began, and I like both of them, because they are oddly parallel. In the middle of the first semester of his freshman year at St. Olaf College (the college where he would later become a professor and where three of his four daughters would be students), he was sitting at a table covered with index cards, on which he had tirelessly recorded the needed information for a term paper he was struggling to write, when his draft notice arrived in the mail. My father told me his first response was "Great! Now I don't have to finish this damned paper." Reading his draft notice, my father didn't look mortality in the face. That would come later. My mother told me that the morning after the Nazi invasion of Norway, April 9, 1940, my grandmother woke up her children by saying, "Get up. It's war." Rather than fear, my mother felt only intense excitement. I have given both of these stories settings in my mind. When I think of my father and his index cards, I see him in a college house where a friend of mine lived when I was a student. It's a false setting. My father didn't live there. I needed a place and I plopped him down in that house unconsciously. I never saw where my mother lived during the war either, but I see my grandmother waking her children in rooms I've cooked up to fill the emptiness. I see morning light through the windows and a white bed where my mother opens her eyes to discover that the German army is on Norwegian soil.

Both of my mother's brothers were in the Norwegian Underground, and I have given their stories settings, too. Neither one of them ever said a word about their involvement, but my mother told me that one day she saw her brother Sverre talking to the schoolteacher in town, and she knew. I see my uncle near a brick building speaking to a short, balding man. My mother never provided these details. They're my own, and I'm sure they're wrong, but the image persists. I have never changed or embellished it in any way. Later in the war, my uncle Sverre got word that the Nazis had been informed of his Underground involvement, and he skied to Sweden to escape. He spent the remaining years of the war there. My mother and her sister took him into the woods and waved good-bye. Again, not a word about where he was going was ever spoken. I see the three of them in the snow among bare trees, a few brown stalks protruding from the snow. My uncle has a backpack and he skis off, propelling himself forward briskly with his poles. Often the origins of such images are untraceable, but sometimes the associative logic at work announces itself after a moment's thought. The chances that the building near which my mother's brother stood was brick is unlikely. The red brick in my mind is conjured from the word *schoolteacher*. All my schools were brick.

And sometimes a detail provided by the teller grows in the mind of the listener, as is the case with potatoes in a story my mother told me. She was jailed by the Germans in Norway for nine days in February after the April invasion. She and a number of other students had protested the occupation in December. Nazi officers came to her school and arrested her. Rather than pay a fine, she chose jail. As my mother has often said, had it been later, the protesters would have been sent to Germany and would probably never have returned; but as she also always adds, had it been later, nobody would have dared protest openly. When I was a child, the idea of my dear, pretty mother in jail filled me with both indignation and pride. My sisters and I were the only children we knew of in Northfield who could boast of having a mother who had been in "jail." She was in a tiny cell with a single, high-barred window, a cot, and a pail for urine and feces—just like in the movies. The food was bad. She told me the potatoes were green through and through. Those potatoes loom in my mind as the signifier of that jail. When I imagine it, everything is in black and white like a photograph, except the potatoes, which glow green in the dim light. After only nine days, she left jail with a bloated stomach.

My father has talked very little about the war. He once said to me that he kept himself sane by telling himself over and over that the whole thing was insane. One story he told me left a deep impression. While he was a soldier in the Philippines, he became ill, so ill that he was finally moved to a collecting station. His memory of those days is vague, because his fever was high, and he passed in and out of consciousness. At the station, however, he woke up and noticed a tag on his chest that said YELLOW FEVER. He had been misdiagnosed. I have always imagined this memory of my father's as if I were my father. I open my eyes and try to orient myself. I am lying on a cot in a makeshift hospital outside, along with other maimed and sick soldiers on stretchers. The tag is yellow. This ludicrous transfer of the name of the illness onto the tag is, I'm sure, nonsense; but my brain is obviously in the business of bald simplification, and that's how I see it. This scene takes place in color. I have certainly borrowed its details from war movies and from what I have seen of Asia, not where my father found himself but farther north, in Thailand and China.

Why I imagine myself inside my father's body in this story and not inside my mother's body when she was jailed is not, I think, accidental. It corresponds to the distinct levels of consciousness in each story—that is, in order to understand what happened to my mother, it is enough to move myself into that jail and see her there. In order to understand what happened to my father, I must imagine waking in a fever and making out the letters that spell out imminent death. I rechecked this story with my father, and he says there was no yellow fever in the Philippines then, and he really doesn't know who made the diagnosis. In reality, he, not the tag, was yellow. He suffered from severe jaundice, a result of having both malaria and hepatitis. Because my father has never shared the other stories, the horrors of combat itself, this experience became for me the quintessential moment of war, a tale of looking at one's own death. It can be argued that accuracy isn't always crucial to understanding. I have never been in jail, and I have never been a soldier, but I imagined these events and places to the extent that it is possible for me, and that imagining has brought me closer to my parents.

After the war, my father finished St. Olaf College on the GI bill, with a lot of other vets who are now legend in the history of the school. A college started by Norwegian immigrants and affiliated with the American Lutheran Church, St. Olaf attracts the mostly well behaved offspring of white middle-class midwesterners, many of them with Norwegian roots. It is not a wild place. Dancing was forbidden until the 1950s. I went to college there, had some wonderful teachers, but the students were by and large a sleepy, complacent lot, more conservative than their professors and easily "managed" by them. My father and his veteran cohorts were not. He tells a story about a man I knew as somebody's highly respectable "dad" literally swinging from the rafters in one of the dormitories. I see him flying above a crowd of heads with a bottle of whiskey. The bottle, however, may well be my embellishment. Four years at war had turned them into men, as the saying goes, and they took the place by storm, not only with their poker games and Tarzan antics but with their intellectual hunger. All this is true, and yet it has taken on the quality of fiction. I read the stories I've been told in my own way and make a narrative of them. Narrative is a chain of links, and I link furiously, merrily hurdling over holes, gaps, and secrets. Nevertheless, I try to remind myself that the holes are there. They are always there, not only in the lives of others but in my own life as well.

The stories and pictures I make for the lives of the people closest to me are the form my empathy takes. My father took the place he knew best and transfigured it, but he has never left it behind. He received his Ph.D. in Scandinavian studies from the University of Wisconsin at Madison. His dissertation, which became a book and was awarded the McKnight Prize for literature, is a biography of Rasmus Bjorn Andersen—an influential figure in the Norwegian American immigrant community. The book is not only the biography of a man but the story of a time and place. My father has used his gifts to understand and preserve "home," not in the narrow sense of that single house with those particular people but in its larger sense of subculture. I think it is fair to argue that his "place"—the world of his childhood, the world I glimpsed in the old people I knew as a child—is now paper. My father has been the secretary of the Norwegian American Historical Association for over thirty years. The association publishes books about immigrant history, but it is also an archive. Over the years, my father has devoted countless hours to organizing what was once unsorted mountains of paper in innumerable boxes and is now an annotated archive of letters, newspapers, diaries, journals, and more. These are facts. What is more interesting is his will to do it, his tireless commitment to the work of piecing together a past. Simple nationalism or chauvinism for a "people" is beside the point. The archive provides information on fools as well as on heroes; it documents both hardy pioneers and those who died or went mad from homesickness. There is a story of a farmer who thought the flatness of the Minnesota land would kill him if he looked at it any longer; unearthing rock after rock, he built his own mountain in memory of the home he had left. My mother felt a natural sympathy for this man, and when a huge rock was dug out of her own yard in Minnesota, she kept it. It's still there—her "Norwegian mountain." When I worked with my father on the annotated bibliography of that archive, I began to understand that his life's work has been the recovery of a place through the cataloging of its particularity—a job that resembles, at least in spirit, the Encyclopedists of the eighteenth century. By its very nature, the catalog dignifies every entry, be it a political tract, a letter, or a cake recipe. Though not necessarily equal in importance, each is part of the story, and there's a democracy to the telling. I think, too, although my father has never told me this, that his work has been for his own father, an act of love through the recovery of place and story.

I remember my grandfather as soft-spoken and, as with my grandmother on my mother's side, I remember his touch. It struck me, even as a child, as unusually tender. There was no brusqueness in him, and I remember that when I showed him my drawings, his sober, quiet face would come alive. He chewed tobacco, and he offered us ribbon candy as a special treat. He lost four fingers to an axe chopping wood, and I recall that the stubs on his hand fascinated but didn't scare me. When I think of him, I remember him in a particular chair in the small living room of his house. He died of a stroke the year I was in Norway: 1973. I was too far away to attend the funeral. We were not a long-distance-telephone family. They wrote me the news. I spoke to my parents once that year on the phone.

3

My first real memory takes place in a bathroom. I remember the tile floor, which is pale, but I can't give it a color. I am walking through the door toward my mother, who is in the bath. I can see the bubbles. I know it's a real memory and not a false one taken from photographs or stories because there are no pictures of that bathroom and because the proportions of the bathtub and toilet correspond to the height of a small person. The bubbles fascinate me, and the presence of my mother fills me with strong, simple pleasure. My mother, who hasn't spent much time in bubble baths during the course of her life, has always been somewhat dubious about this memory. But within this isolated fragment I see the path of my walk—the hallway, small living area, the door to the kitchen; and when I described the walk to my mother, she confirmed that the rooms correspond to the graduate-student barracks near the University of Wisconsin at Madison. I was three.

I have memories of that first trip to Norway, too. The most striking is one of light and color. I am sitting outside at a table with my sister and my mother and my aunt. My cousins were probably there as well, but I have no memory of them. The sunshine is so brilliant I have to squint. We are close to water. I have no idea whether it was a fjord near Bergen or the ocean off Mandal. It's water and it's blue. It's probably the fjord, because I do not remember vastness or a beach but trees and rocks. The table is white, and on the table are glasses of shining soda pop— yellow and red. Those glasses of *brus* (the Norwegian word for soda pop, a word I never forgot) delight and fascinate me. I am quite sure that I'd never seen red soda before, and the memory is so powerful, I must have felt I was in the presence of a Norwegian miracle. That bottle of red *brus* on a white table gleamed throughout the remaining years of my childhood as the sign of what was possible *there*. It may have been in part responsible for the question I asked my mother when I was five or six: "Why is everything better in Norway?" I don't remember asking the question, but my mother assures me I was tactless enough to ask it. My poor mother decided that she had framed her emigration in the wrong light and vowed to be more careful about her comparisons between the two countries in the future.

Early memories are isolated bits of experience remembered for reasons that are often difficult to articulate; and because they have no greater narrative in which they can be framed, they float. At the same time, they may have more purity than later memories, for that very reason. When dailiness enters memory, repetition fixes places in the mind, but it also burdens them with a wealth of experience that is often difficult to untangle. For example, I remember Longfellow School, where I attended grade school, very well. I can see its hallways and connect one to another. I can even see the bathroom outside my third-grade class. I remember it as gray. It may have been gray, but it could be that I colored it in memory. I have given the interior of that building a single color that is also emotional: gray. Although I was always excited to begin school in the fall (a season separated from the spring before by years of summer), and although I loved walking out to the school-bus with my three sisters, wearing the identical new dresses my mother had sewn for us, my memory of the school building itself, its rooms and lockers, blackboards, and hallways, brings on a heavy, oppressive feeling. Whether I was more unhappy in school than any of my friends, I don't know. I never would have said I didn't like school, and there are moments I distinctly remember enjoying, but these truths don't alter my memory of that place. There's something unpleasant about saying that a gut response can be a lie, but I think it's possible. Unlike the intricacy of the physical world, feelings are generally more crude than language—guilt, shame, being hurt by another person feel remarkably alike in the body. Reason tells me that my early experiences in that school were a complex mixture of pain, pleasure, and boredom, but whenever I drive past it or think about it, the building itself is wrapped in gloom.

Many years later, I had a similar experience but in reverse. From 1978 through 1986, I was a graduate student at Columbia, but by 1981 I had met my future husband and moved first to SoHo, in downtown Manhattan, and then to Brooklyn. It is true that those first couple of years, when I was living near Columbia, I was very poor. It is true that I suffered in a difficult and stupid love affair, and that I worked in one bad job after another to try to keep myself going. Nevertheless, I remember that time as extraordinary, and I wouldn't trade it for anything. I don't even wish now that I had had more money. And had I been asked if I was suffering at the time, I would have said a defiant *no*. After I left that neighbor-hood, however, I rarely returned to it. I saw my dissertation adviser three times in three years and then defended on a clear spring day in 1986. After that, I disappeared for good. Several years later, I returned, because my husband, Paul Auster, had been asked to give a talk at the Maison Française. Walking across campus made me feel sad, and I thought to myself, I wasn't happy here. Then after the reading, we walked past Butler Library. It was dark, but the light inside illuminated the windows. Students were reading and working, and those lit windows gave me a wonderful, weightless feeling. I understood for the first time how happy I had been there—in the library. Butler is a good library, one of the best. It has some handsome rooms, but its stacks are inhospitable and dark. One spring while I was a student, all the women were given whistles before they entered the stacks, because an exhibitionist had been prowling the badly lit corridors, and we were told to pucker up and blow if there was any trouble. Again, I don't fully understand my emotional response to that library or trust it. It was the site of a series of intellectual revelations that were crucial to me, not just as a student but as a human being. I read Sigmund Freud in that library and Emile Benveniste and Roman Jakobson and Mikhail Bakhtin and was forever changed by them, but I also sweated out bad papers and was bored and troubled and irritated there. My mind wandered from the work at hand and strayed to food or clothes I couldn't afford or to the attractive arms and shoulders of some young man sitting at the far end of the table. So what does it mean that the sight of Butler Library turned me into a quivering heap of sentimental mush? It can only be that places left behind often become emotionally simplified—that they sound a single note of pain or pleasure, which means that they are never what they were.

At the same time, I'm fully aware that libraries occupy a particular place in my life, and my sudden burst of feeling for Butler isn't related only to my life as a graduate student. My father took me and my sisters into the dim, dusty stacks on the seventh floor of Rolvaag Library at St. Olaf, where he worked for the historical association. To get there, we walked into an old elevator with a bright red door and a grate that folded and unfolded with lots of creaking and banging. I was already a heroine then, Alice or Pollyanna or a generic princess from a fairy tale—and the trip into that landscape of book spines and bad light made me feel like a person in a story on some curious adventure. It may be that I link every library to that first one—to my early childhood experience of drawing on the floor near my father's desk. A library is of course a real place, but it is also an unreal one. What happens there is mostly silent. I think I've always liked the whispering aspect of libraries, the hushing librarians and my feeling of solitude among many. When her children were older, my mother worked part-time in the St. Olaf library, too. She was employed there when I was a student. I didn't sleep in Rolvaag Library, but most of my waking hours were spent in a carrel there, and sometimes she would come to see me. I would feel her hands on my shoulders and turn my head, knowing I was going to see my mother. Years before she found herself filing periodicals in that library, she found books for me. It was my Norwegian mother, not my American father, who introduced me to the English poems and novels that affected me most when I was young. She gave me Blake's *Songs of Innocence and Experience* when I was eleven. I didn't understand those poems, but they fascinated me as much as *Alice in Wonderland* had, and I read them again and again with mingled horror and pleasure. She gave me Emily Dickinson, too, around the same time, a tiny green edition of famous poems, and I would repeat those poems to myself in a trance. They were secrets to me, strange and private. I think it was the sound of those poems that I loved. I chewed on Blake's and Dickinson's words like food. I ate them, even when their meanings eluded me.

It was my mother who sent me off to the library for *David Copperfield* and *Jane Eyre* and *Wuthering Heights* when I was thirteen, and it's fair to say that to this day I have not recovered from a single one of those novels. That was the summer of 1968, and my family was in Iceland. I cannot think of Reykjavik without the thought that I was David and Jane and Catherine there in that house, where I found it hard to sleep, because the sun never set. I would go to the window and lift the shade in the bedroom and look out into the eerie light that fell over the roofs, not daylight at all, some other light I had never seen before and have never seen since. The otherworldly landscape of Iceland has come to mean story for me. My father took us out into the countryside to the places where the sagas are said to have taken place. The sagas are fiction, but their settings are geographically exact. I will never forget my father stopping the Volkswagen bug we had rented; and after all six of us had piled out of that tiny car, and we stood on that treeless ground with its black lava rock and smoking geisers and green lichen, my father showed us where Snorre died. "The axe fell on him here!" And when my father said it, I saw the blood running on the ground. When he wasn't finding the sites where the heroes had wandered, my father was in the library reading about them. The very idea of a library for me is bound to my mother and father and includes the history of my own metamorphoses through books, fictions that are no less part of me than much of my own history.

4

Seventy-six years after Uncle David walked off the ship at Ellis Island, I arrived at the airport in New York City. It was early September 1978. I didn't know a living soul in the place. My suitcase was heavy, and nobody helped me carry it, something unheard of in Minneapolis. But frankly, even this indifference from New Yorkers didn't bother me. I had left small-town, rural life for good, and I had no intention of ever returning, not because I didn't like my home but because I had always known that I would leave. Leaving was part of my life romance, part of an idea I had about myself as a person destined for adventure; and as far as I could tell, adventure lay in the urban wilds of Manhattan, not in the farmland of Minnesota. This was my guiding fiction, and I was determined to make good on it. I had a tiny room in International House, on West 123rd Street at Harlem's border. My first three days were spent rereading *Crime and Punishment* in a state that closely resembled fever. I couldn't sleep, because the noise from traffic, sirens, garbage trucks, and exuberant pedestrians outside my window kept me wide awake all night. I had no friends. Was I happy? I was wildly happy. Sitting on my bed, which took up most of the space in that narrow room, I whispered prayers of thanks that I was really and truly *here* in New York, beginning another life. I worshiped the place. I feasted on every beautiful inch of it—the crowds, the fruit and vegetable stands, the miles of pavement, the graffiti, even the garbage. All of it sent me into paroxysms of joy. Needless to say, my elation had an irrational cast to it. Had I not arrived laden with ideas of urban paradise, I might have felt bad losing sleep, might have felt lonely and disoriented, but instead I walked around town like a love-struck idiot, inhaling the difference between *there* and *here*. I had never seen anything like New York, and its newness held the promise of my future: dense with the experience I craved—romantic, urbane, intellectual. Looking back on that moment, I believe I was saved from disappointment by the nature of my "great expectations." I honestly wasn't burdened with conventional notions of finding security or happiness. At that time of my life, even when I was "happy," it wasn't because I expected it. That was for characters less romantic than myself. I didn't expect to be rich, well fed, and kindly treated by all. I wanted to live deeply and fully, to embrace whatever the city held for me, and if this meant a few emotional bruises, even a couple of shocks, if it meant not eating too well or too often, if it meant a whole slew of awful jobs, so be it.

It appears that time has turned that young woman, who imagined herself a romantic heroine, into something of a comic character, but I remain fond of her. We are relatives, after all. Like all the places where I've actually lived, New York City is much more than a "context" or "setting" for me. Within weeks of my arrival in New York, I was someone else, not because there had been a revolution in my psychological makeup or any trauma. It was simply this: people saw me in a light in which I had never been seen before. Although I had always felt at home with my parents and sisters, I was never really comfortable with my peers. By the time I found myself in college, my feeling that I was not inside but outside had intensified. There's no question that I cultivated this to some degree, that I prided myself on my difference, but I confess it hurt and surprised me to be regarded as "strange." I had friends I loved and teachers I loved, but rumors in which I was variously characterized as wild, monkishly studious, or just plain weird haunted my career as a college student. I recall my father telling me with a smile that one of his students had described me as "very unique." In New York, this all but ended. Whatever exoticism I may have possessed came from my midwestern sincerity and lack of worldly sophistication. Transformations of the self are related to *where* you are, and identity *is* dependent on others. In Minnesota, I felt embattled. I rebelled against a culture that touted "niceness" above truth, that wallowed in an idea of "equality" that had come to mean "sameness" and "intolerance"—not of the sick, dying, ugly, or handicapped but of those who distinguished themselves by talent or beauty or intelligence. The "hoity-toity" were really batted around out there. Pretension wasn't suffered for an instant, and for a girl who walked around dreaming she was a combination of George Eliot and Nora Charles in *The Thin Man*, life could be hard. In Minnesota, I lusted after every quality that was in short supply—artifice, irony, flamboyant theatricality, fierce intellectual debate, and brilliantly painted lips. (I went for the lips.)

In New York, "niceness" wasn't an overriding value, but then neither was "goodness," a value I frankly and unashamedly clung to for dear life. I had to reorient myself to accommodate a new world. For example, I naively assumed that most people had had some kind of religious education, that religion remained a fact of most people's lives and provided the ground for moral life. I was startled to discover, however, when we were assigned the first book of the Bible for a literature class, that a majority of my fellow students had never read Genesis. Nevertheless, I wasn't an "odd duck" in New York, the city that accommodates or ignores all ducks. And despite the harshness of everyday life—the raw, cold, scraping sensation of never leaving the street, because my apartment felt as if it were *in* the street—I was at home in New York. This feeling of being "home at last" corresponds to my idea about the city, an idea shaped by books, movies, and plays, an idea of infinite possibility.

There is an incident, however, that made me understand what New York is for the people who come here to stay. I had been living in Manhattan for two years. I had met my future husband, and we were invited to a dinner at Westbeth—the housing project in the West Village for artists. It was a lovely dinner, and I was delighted to be there in that company. I was in love. I was happy

without having sought happiness. I vaguely remember wearing
something silly, but no one minded. Everyone at the table looked
like a marvel to me, but there was one man in particular who
shone that night. It seemed to me that he had stepped right out of
a Noël Coward play. His jokes were witty, his repartee sharp, and
his manner nonchalant. He had written a book on Andy Warhol—
no surprise. He was the most urbane creature I had ever laid eyes
on. And I laughed and smiled and felt like Miranda: "How beau-
teous mankind is. O brave new world that has such people in't."
The conversation wandered, as conversations do, and people began
to talk about where they had grown up. Nobody, if I remember
correctly, had been born and raised in New York City, and where
had my idol sprung from, this divinity of culture and wit? Where
had he spent his entire childhood and youth? In Northfield, Minnesota. I hadn't known him, because he is several years older than
I am, but there it was: he and I had grown up in the same small
town. New York City is the place where people come to invent,
reinvent, or find the room they need to be who they wish to be.
It's a place where fictions run freely and plentifully, where people
are allowed a certain pretense about themselves, where cultivating
a persona or an idea of how to live is permitted, even encouraged.
This is the glory of urban freedom and indifference. It has its
drawbacks, of course. One summer I was alone in New York. All
my friends had fled the city heat, and I remember thinking, If I
died right now in my apartment, how long would it take before
anybody noticed?

I now live in Brooklyn, the place that nobody visits but where
lots of people live. It is more ethnically diverse than Manhattan.
The buildings are lower. We have more trees. I have zealously
attached myself to my neighborhood, Park Slope, and defend it
loyally. But all the time I've lived in Brooklyn, I've been writing

about other places. I wrote a book called *The Blindfold* here, about a young graduate student who lives near Columbia and has a number of peculiar adventures. She and I aren't the same person, but she's close to me. And I put her in my old apartment, the one I rented on West 109th Street. When I wrote her stories, I saw her in my apartment and on the streets I knew so well. What she did wasn't what I had done, but I don't think I could have written that book had I not put her there, and I couldn't have written it had I still been living in that building.

5

Long before I had heard about the New Critics or structuralism or deconstruction, teachers liked to talk about "setting" as one of the elements of fiction. It went along with "theme" and "character." I can't remember how Paul and I started our discussion of place in fiction or how we arrived at his startling comment about *Pride and Prejudice*. But I clearly remember him saying that Austen's novel had taken place in his parents' living room in New Jersey. Although any self-respecting junior high school teacher would have scoffed at such a remark about "setting," I realized I had done the same thing while reading Céline's novel *Death on the Installment Plan*. When Ferdinand finally takes refuge in his uncle's house, I imagined him in my paternal grandparents' little white house outside of Cannon Falls. Ferdinand says, "Yes Uncle," in the small bedroom on the ground floor off the living room. The disparities between a gentry drawing room in England in the late eighteenth century and a suburban living room in New Jersey in the middle of the twentieth, or the ones between the French countryside in the early part of this century and the rural Midwest, are obvious. What is remarkable to me is that I had to think about it to know what I had done. When you read, you see. The images aren't manufactured with effort. They simply appear to you through the experience of the text and are rarely questioned. The pictures conjured are enough to push you forward and are to a large extent, I think, like my image of the word *yonder*. They serve a function. And like the picture I carry with me of my uncle talking to his colleague in the Underground, they are not fully fleshed out. Although I can imagine my uncle's face because I knew him when he was alive, the schoolteacher is a blur except for his bald head.

Fictional characters are not constantly trampling over home territory in my mind, however. Often the source of the image is less clear. *Middlemarch* is a book I've read several times, and when Dorothea is in Rome with Casaubon, I always have the same picture of it. This is significant, because I read the book both before and after I actually visited Rome, and the real city didn't disturb in any way the imaginary one I had provided for Dorothea. Eliot's Rome in *Middlemarch* is for me essentially a stage set. The walls of the empty and dead city are built of cardboard that has been painted to look like stone. While the image is wrongheaded in some way, what I see is architecture as metaphor. Dorothea's terrible mistake is that she sees truth and power in what is false and impotent, and my artificial Rome extends the discovery of her wedding trip to the city where it occurs. Every time I read anything, I loot the world with luxurious abandon, robbing from real places and unreal ones, snatching images from movies, from postcards and paintings and even cartoons. And when I think of a book, especially one that is dear to me, I see those stolen places again, and they move me. There is a reason, after all, why Paul imagined the elaborate social intercourse and moral drama of Austen in his parents' living room. It was clearly the site for him of similar exchanges. Things happened in that living room. As for why Ferdinand's final refuge in the country belongs to my grandparents' house, it is for me the place of my father, and after that poor boy's ridiculous and heartbreaking adventures, he finds comfort at last from a paternal figure—his uncle.

The place of reading is a kind of yonder world, a place that is neither here nor there but made up of the bits and pieces of experience in every sense, both real and fictional, two categories that become harder to separate the more you think about them. When I was doing research for a professor as a graduate student, a job that paid my tuition and fees, I read excerpts from diaries recorded during Captain Cook's legendary voyages. On the expedition, both captain and crew saw a volcano. This volcano was described separately by Cook himself and by a young man aboard ship. The difference between those descriptions astonished me. Cook reports on the volcano in the cool, scientific prose of the Enlightenment, but the young man describes the same sight in rapturous tones already coded by Romanticism. The two looked in the same direction, but they didn't see the same event. Each had his own language for seeing, and that language created his vision. We all inherit vision just as they did—two men who stood side by side but were nevertheless separated by an intellectual chasm. It is almost impossible for us as residents of the Western world to imagine a pre-Romantic view of nature. My feeling for mountainous western Norway, undoubtedly shaped by the history of my family there, is also influenced by Romanticism. People simply don't see mountains as annoying impasses anymore. They breathe in the air and beat their breasts and drink in the beauty of the rugged landscape, but where does this come from, if not from the Romantics, who took up crags and cliffs as the shape of the sublime? No place is naked. It may be that in infancy we experience the nakedness of place, but without memory it remains inaccessible.

After my daughter was born, I flew around the apartment where I lived, in the grip of a new mother's euphoria. I couldn't look at my darling's tiny face enough, couldn't see it enough, and I had to creep into her room when she napped just to stare down at her in stupefied awe. But when I looked at her, I often wondered what the world was like from her point of view. She didn't know where she began or ended, didn't know that the toes she found so entertaining belonged to her. But connections come fast for babies. Meanings are made early through the presence and absence of the mother, through the cry answered, the smile answered, through sounds that are not language but like language, and then words themselves appear as a response to what is missing. Now that she's eight, Sophie lives in a world so dense with shaping fictions that her father and I are continually amused. She's a poor woman with a scarf around her head and a begging cup. She's a country-and-western singer, drawling out lyrics about lost love. She's Judy Garland in an obscure musical called *Summer Stock*. She's Pippi. She's Anne of Green Gables. She's a mother with a vengeance, changing, burping, waking the angel from naps, cooing and singing and patting and strolling her. The "baby" is life-size, plastic, and made in France.

For all the radical persona experimentation we call "play," children are placemongers. More than adults, they like to stay put, and they like order in the form of repetition. They attach themselves fiercely to houses, rooms, and familiar objects, and change is frowned upon. The son of a close friend of Paul's and mine is a case in point. For years he lived with his painter father in a loft in downtown Manhattan. The bathroom in their loft was a sad affair with broken flooring. When the father started earning more money from his work, he renovated the bathroom. His son mourned. "That old bathroom floor was my friend." Parents often discover that their redecorating schemes are anathema to their children. My daughter has moved just once in her eight years, from a small apartment in Brooklyn to a large brownstone a block and a half away. When we showed her the new house, she didn't like it. She worried about the strange furniture in it. I think she imagined that the people from whom we bought the house would leave their things, and all those unfamiliar objects made her uncomfortable. Then she had to survive the painting of the house, including her room, which took a couple of weeks, and she didn't like that either. But once she had settled herself there, and had arranged her toys, she glued herself to that place and has invested it with all the affection she felt for her old room. The power of forms—spatial and verbal—as needed orientation in life can hardly be overestimated.

And every night I read to her. We have made our way through innumerable books, all fourteen *Oz* books, five *Anne* books, the Narnia series, all the Moomintroll books, E. Nesbitt and Lloyd Alexander and fairy tales from all over the world. Reading is a ritual which is itself associated with place, an event that happens after her teeth have been brushed and before she sleeps. No matter how harrowing the tales or how deep the identification (Sophie gasps, shudders, and, on occasion, sobs loudly during our reading), her body at least is securely in its bed. It may be that the singularity of place within the ritual is exactly what makes the sadness, fear, and excitement of these stories not only bearable but pleasurable. Repetition within ritual creates order through time, and repeating the form brings stability. As children my sisters and I cultivated the holiday rituals in our house to a degree that bordered on the fanatical. We still do. Every year, we—and that now includes three Jewish husbands and a lone Protestant, as well as five offspring—reenact the Christmas ritual at my parents' house in Minnesota. The sequence of celebration is written in stone and has never altered. From the bringing in of the *Jul* log to the food, to dancing and singing around the Christmas tree, the event unfolds as it always has. Age may have made us more flexible in theory, but in practice our Christmas is as predictable as the sunrise, and we love it wholeheartedly. My parents moved to that house outside Northfield when I was in the third grade, and they have lived there ever since. The clothes my sisters and I wore for "dress-up" can still be found in the same box. Many people move from place to place, but my parents didn't. That house holds my childhood with them and with Liv and Astrid and Ingrid, and I think the very idea of that place has given us a sense of ground, order, and continuity that is more rare than common. And that indisputable firmness of place is what allowed us all to go far away. For several years, Liv lived in Hong Kong, Astrid in Paris, and Ingrid and I were in New York.

The desire for coherence and order is human. Nonsense and chaos wreck people as surely as a terrible beating. And nonsense and chaos are everywhere. The self exists in time and space: the narrative of the self in memory and a continuity of place in "home." My stepson, Daniel, who is now eighteen, does not remember living in one place with both of his parents. That is a paradise lost. Although one might imagine "two homes" as a doubling of the comforts of home, real experience doesn't bear this out. The old expression, now out of fashion, "a broken home" comes closer to the truth. Children, especially, long for wholeness, for unity, perhaps because they are closer to that early, fragmentary state before any "self" is formed, or perhaps because they are truly not the masters of their destinies. And although divorce is commonplace enough and often benign—without open rancor between parents—going from *here* to *there* can become a form of being *nowhere*. The child finds himself *yonder* in a land between father and mother. Because "home" is more than a place to park the body, because it is necessarily a symbolic landscape, what can it mean to have two of them? Two homes inevitably contradict each other, always in small ways, sometimes in big ones. What happens if the words spoken in one place contradict the words in the other? Where does the child reside then? And what does it mean for that child's relations to the symbolic world in general— to language itself as the expression of truth, of all meaning? When Daniel was in the second grade, he invented a place he called the "Half-World." I think it was in outer space, and all the people who lived in it were literally cut in two. He wasn't old enough to know why he had concocted this place, but when he told me about it, I suffered a sharp, terrible pang of recognition. I asked him if those people could ever be put back together again. He said yes. And I think he was right. There are ways to sew the Half-World together again, even though it is impossible to change its torn history. Daniel takes photographs, and some of them are remarkable. Many of them are images of places he has isolated in ways I would never have imagined. When I look at his shadows cast on sidewalks, his mirror images in windows, the cracks and ruined lines on his doors of abandoned houses, or the invasive vines that blur the architecture of a small building, I know that these pictures are threads of himself. He sews with his camera and in the darkroom. And no matter how derelict his subjects are, there is radiant order to each and every picture. They are precisely framed. Every line, every shadow is exactly where he wants it to be.

A photograph of a place is not a real place any more than a book is, but we inhabit photographs nevertheless as spectator or as identifying actor. Words are more abstract than images, but images are inevitably born of them. The pictorial drama of reading corresponds to the one of writing. You cannot have one without the other. Reading is active, but writing is more active. Making fiction is making a place for the reader in the text, and this brings up the eternal question of making a book: what to put in and what to leave out. One can argue that there are two kinds of writers in the world: the ones who put it all in and the ones who leave a lot of it out. Sweeping claims can be made about history and these impulses. Inclusion and volume can be understood as a literary idea that was begun in the eighteenth century, developed in the nineteenth, and lasted through Joyce. (He may have turned literature on its head but he kept a lot in.) Exclusion, too, can be seen as essential to late modernism, most notably Kafka and Beckett. But these are not useful categories "here." (The reader is "here" with me if he or she has come so far.) There are times when a detailed description of a living room and all its furnishings is annoying, when it gets in the way of reading, and then there are times when it does not. Austen is spare in description. Had she described every object in the Bennet parlor, Paul never would have squeezed in his New Jersey living room among all that clutter, and it seems to me the moral resonance of that book would have been partly lost. On the other hand, I cannot imagine Dickens without his full descriptions of places—the stinking Thames and Mr. Venus's ghastly workshop in *Our Mutual Friend*, for example; but these descriptions, like Sterne's clock in *Tristram Shandy*, are always to a purpose. They accelerate the book. They don't bog it down in pointless novelistic gab. Good books usually say enough about where they happen, but not too much. Enough can be more or less, but it's bad books that treat the reader to his expectations about what a novel or a story or a poem is or *where* it is. There is something comforting about bad books, which is why people read them. Surprise can be a wonderful thing, but, on the whole, people don't want it, any more than most children want their rooms changed. They want what they already know to be confirmed, and they have been richly supplied with these fictional comforts since the late eighteenth century, when the novel became popular with the rise in mass literacy. But the good reader (a quality not at all determined by literary sophistication) wants room to fill in the blanks. Every reader writes the book he or she reads, supplying what isn't there, and that creative invention becomes the book.

For the past four years I've been writing a novel set in my hometown, or rather in a fictional version of Northfield. The town in the book is not the real town, but it resembles it strongly. It has another name, Webster, and although it resembles the real town, its geography is askew. I have taken real places—the Ideal Cafe, the Stuart Hotel, Tiny's Smoke Shop, the Cannon River, and Heath Creek, with their names intact—but I relocated some of these places and gave them new inhabitants. Oddly enough, these changes weren't made for my convenience, and I didn't make them without seeing them in my mind first. The collapsing and shifting of that known landscape came about because it "felt right." The map of fictional Webster isn't identical to the map of Northfield, because the one departs emotionally from the other. Since I began writing the book, I have been back to Northfield several times, every Christmas and once during the summer.

When I walk past the Ideal Cafe, where Lily Dahl, the heroine of my book, works, I don't feel much. I find myself looking closely at it, examining the windows on the second floor, behind which is Lily's imaginary apartment, but it just isn't the place I made for myself in fiction. That place exists in memory, but it isn't "real" memory. My best friend, Heather Clark, and my sisters Liv and Astrid all worked in the Ideal Cafe in the 1970s, when it was in its heyday, and they told me stories about their customers that I have never forgotten. I stole some of them. I have eaten breakfast and lunch and wolfed down pieces of pie in the Ideal Cafe, and I think I remember pretty well what it looked like when I was in high school, but the imaginary cafe where Lily works has supplanted the one I remember and become more "real" to me. Writing fiction is like remembering what never happened. It mimics memory without being memory. Images appear as textual ground, because this is how the brain works. Ignorant as I am of the science of memory and the brain, I am convinced that the processes of memory and invention are linked in the mind. Homer evokes the muse of memory before beginning his tale. And the ancient memory systems developed to enhance recollection were always rooted to places. The speaker wandered through houses in his mind, either real or invented, and located words in its various rooms and objects. Cicero articulated an architecture of memory dependent on spaces that were well lit. Murky, cramped little hovels wouldn't do as spatial tools for recollection. Every new draft of a book is the work not only of shrinking and expanding and shrinking again but of finding the book's truth, which means throwing out the lies that tempt me. This work is like dredging up a memory that's been obscured by some comfortable delusion and forcing it "to light," a process that can be excruciating. Fiction exists in the borderland of dream and memory. Like dreams, it distorts for its own purpose, sometimes consciously, sometimes unconsciously, and, like memory, fiction requires an effort of concentration to recall how it *really* was. There have been a few extraordinary books written in the present tense, but by and large it's an awkward form. Fiction usually takes place in the past. Somehow that's its natural place.

Paul often says that it's a strange business, this sitting alone in a room making up people and places, and that in the long run, nobody does it unless he has to. Years ago, he translated a French writer, Joseph Joubert, whose brief but startling journal entries have become part of our ongoing dialogue about art. Joubert wrote: "Those for whom the world is not enough: poets, philosophers and all lovers of books." When I read *Death on the Installment Plan* in my early thirties, the book in which I imagined the hero in my grandparents' house, I loved it so much I was sorry to finish it. I closed the book and shocked myself by thinking, "This is better than life." I didn't mean or want to think this, but I'm afraid I did. Certainly this feeling about a book is the one that makes people want to write. I don't know why I feel more alive when I write, but I do. Maybe I imagine that if I scratch hard enough into the paper, I will last. Maybe the world isn't enough, or maybe the distinction between the world and fiction is not so clear. Fiction is made from the stuff of the world, after all, which includes dreams and wishes and fantasies and memory. And it is never really made alone, but from the material between and among us: language. When Mikhail Bakhtin argues that the novel is dialogical—multivoiced, conflicted, in constant dialogue within itself—he is identifying all those jabbering voices every fiction writer hears in his or her head. Writing novels is a solitary act that is also plural, and its many voices are forever placing us somewhere—here or there or yonder.

At the same time, writing collapses these spatial categories. Like a heartbeat or a breath, it marks the time of a living consciousness on the page, a consciousness that is present and here, but also absent. The page can resurrect what's lost and what's dead, what's not there anymore and what was never there. Fiction is like the ghost twin of memory that moves through the myriad cities, landscapes, houses, and rooms of the mind.

Vermeer's Annunciation

Every painting is always two paintings: the one you see and the one you remember, which is also to say that every painting worth talking about reveals itself over time and takes on its own story inside the viewer. With Vermeer's work, that story probably lasts as long as the person who sees it. This is my own unfinished story of looking at one of his paintings. Before I walked through the doors of the National Gallery of Art in Washington to look at its historic gathering of twenty-one of Vermeer's works, I hadn't decided which painting I would write about. My job was to discuss only one, and while I was paging through the catalog and listening to the museum officials and curators talk about the show, I turned to *Woman with a Pearl Necklace*. I had never seen the original, although I had admired it in reproduction many times, but suddenly, for reasons I didn't fully understand, this painting of a woman holding up a necklace in the light of a window jumped out at me. Although I didn't have the slightest notion of what I would say about it, the choice had been made, and I walked up the stairs already in its grip.

I spent four hours in the gallery, two of which were spent solely in front of *Woman with a Pearl Necklace*. I looked at it from close up. I looked at it from several feet away. I looked at it from either side. I counted drops of light and scribbled down the numbers. I recorded the painting's elements, working to decipher the murky folds of the large cloth in the foreground. I noted the woman's hands, her orange ribbon, her earring, the yellow of her ermine-trimmed jacket, the mirror frame, the light. I never touched the painting, of course, but once I was reprimanded by a guard. Perhaps my nose came too close to the paint or perhaps my obsessive focus on one painting struck him as slightly deranged. He waved me off, and I made an attempt to look less awed and more professional. There was a bench in that room, and after my dance of distances, I sat down on it and looked at the canvas for a long time. The more I looked at it, the more it overwhelmed me with a feeling of fullness and mystery. I knew what I was looking at, and yet I didn't know. I had to ask myself what I was seeing and why it had become an experience so powerful, I felt I couldn't have lasted another hour without crying. It seemed to me that both because of and despite its particularity, *Woman with a Pearl Necklace* was something other than what it appeared to be. This is an odd statement to make about a painting, which is literally "appearance," and yet I couldn't help feeling that the mystery of the painting was pulling me beyond that room and its solitary woman.

Every viewing of a painting is private, an experience between the spectator and the image, and yet I would wager that the feelings evoked by this painting are remarkably similar, particularly for those who aren't burdened with historical interpretations and the problem of puzzling out Vermeer's intentions. Even the most cursory glance at Vermeer scholarship suggests that there is much disagreement. But I am not an art historian, and those disputes won't come into the story until later. My intention that day was simply to look at this painting, to study it with fresh eyes, and to let the painting and only the painting direct my thoughts. In that gallery in the museum, I looked at the profile of a young woman who is apparently looking at herself in a small mirror. The mirror is only slightly larger than her own face and is represented by its frame only. In fact, the viewer assumes there is glass in the frame only because of the way the woman stands and gazes toward it. But what we imagine she is seeing—her own face—is not part of the painting. The window is so close to the mirror, and its light so clear and dominant on the canvas, that whether she is transfixed by the mirror or by the window isn't entirely clear. My first impression of the painting was that she was looking at the window, although the longer I looked at it, the less sure I became. The woman's gaze is not dreamy but active, the focus of her eyes direct; and although her feet cannot be seen under the shadowed folds of her skirt, they seem to be firmly planted on the floor. Her soft lips aren't smiling, but there is the barest upward tilt at the visible corner of her mouth. And yet there is no feeling that she is about to smile or that her expression will change anytime soon. Her hands aren't moving either. She isn't tying the necklace. She has stopped in mid-gesture and is standing motionless. One look at *The Lacemaker* (also in the show), a painting in which a girl's fingers are caught in action, confirmed for me that the hands of the woman with the pearls are frozen. In fact, the painting is stillness itself—a woman alone and motionless in a room. I am looking in at her solitude, and she cannot see me.

In a number of Vermeer's paintings, the spectator is seen. *Girl with a Red Hat* and *Girl with a Pearl Earring* (both in the Washington show) are paintings in which the spectator and the subject exchange looks, and although neither of these paintings is large, each depicts a partial rather than a whole body. We see only the upper body of the girl with the hat, and only the head and shoulder of the girl with the earring. This focus on faces creates intimate access into the painting for the viewer—two faces meet for what becomes an eternal moment. On the other hand, the woman with the necklace doesn't acknowledge the presence of any onlookers, and the viewer is barred from entrance to the room on two counts. First, the small size of the painting, which holds her entire body, places her in another perspective from that of the onlooker: my dimensions are radically different from hers. And second, the entire foreground of the painting—a large chair and a table draped with dark cloth and topped with a gleaming black covered jar—would have to be shoved aside before anyone from the viewer's position could even imagine stepping into the luminous space she occupies.

So what's happening in this room? The woman trying on her necklace is young, pretty, and beautifully dressed, but she is not preening in front of her reflection. Nothing about her expression or posture suggests vanity. On the table, it is possible to see part of a bowl and a powder brush, but these objects, even if she has recently used them, are forgotten things. They are pulled into the shadow of the dark foreground, which forbids entrance and makes the empty space of light between the woman and mirror more dramatic. While I was looking at the painting, I realized that I had picked it because of its empty center, a quality that distinguished it from other, related works. The painting was hanging in a room with three other great Vermeer paintings of women alone: *Woman in Blue Reading a Letter*, *Young Woman with a Water Pitcher*, and *Woman Holding a Balance*. In all of these paintings, women occupy a space that is illuminated by a far window on the left as you face the canvas (although the window in *Woman in Blue* is implied, rather than depicted, by the source of light that illuminates her page). In the three other paintings there is a map or painting somewhere on the wall in the room. In *Woman with a Pearl Necklace* there is nothing but light.

It turns out that Vermeer changed his mind. Arthur Wheelock, in his short essay on the painting in the catalog, which I read fitfully while I was in the museum, writes that neutron autoradiography of the canvas shows that there was once a map on that shining wall and, moreover, a musical instrument, probably a lute, sitting on the chair. The great folds of cloth in the foreground also covered considerably less of the tile floor. By simplifying the painting, by allowing fewer elements to remain, Vermeer altered the work's effect and meaning forever. The map, which can be seen in the neutron autoradiograph reproduced in the catalog, was located behind the woman's upper body, and even in the small and foggy picture in the catalog, the map draws the viewer back to the wall and gives that surface greater dimension and flatness. By eliminating the map, Vermeer got rid of an object that would have made a geometric cut between the woman's eyes and the window. The map would have interrupted the line of her gaze and disturbed its directness. And had it remained, it would inevitably have called to mind a geography beyond that room, the possibility of travel—of the outside. In the painting's final form, the outside is represented only by light. The instrument would have evoked music, and even the suggestion of sound would have changed the painting, distracting the viewer from its profound hush. By increasing the size of the cloth in the foreground, Vermeer further protected the woman from intrusion. This technology of looking through a painting and exposing it like a palimpsest gives a rare glimpse into art as a movement toward something that is not always known at the outset. As he worked, Vermeer's idea about what he was doing was transformed by what he himself saw, and what he saw during the process and came to paint was something simpler and more sacred than what he had imagined to begin with.

But the question remains: Why is this woman so endlessly fascinating, and how does the painting work its magic on the viewer? Many people feel this is clear, but they explain it differently. In his book *Éloge du Quotidien* (Paris, 1993), Tzvetan Todorov both includes and exempts Vermeer from his subject: daily life in Dutch painting of the period. He argues that by being the highest example of this genre, Vermeer's work transcends it; that because the everyday is taken to another level, it ceases to be everyday. Notably, he tells his reader to look "again and again" at *Woman with a Pearl Necklace*. The ordinary act of trying on a necklace in front of a mirror doesn't look ordinary at all. Vermeer, he says, uses genre themes but doesn't submit to them. I would take this further and say that while *Woman with a Pearl Necklace* uses the Vanitas theme as a point of departure, linking it to other paintings of the period showing women at their toilet, Vermeer subverts the theme. This subversion creates ambiguity, and ambiguity creates fascination. Ambiguity in Vermeer, however, is strangely untroubling. This isn't the uneasy ambiguity of Henry James, for example, where conflicting desires hang in precarious balance or secret motives are buried in appearances. And it isn't the moral ambiguity that Todorov writes about in paintings of the same period in which moments of ethical indecision are depicted. Vermeer presents the viewer with a painting that resembles other paintings about vanity, and since he lived inside the world of painting and painters, this is clearly intentional; but to assume that the painting must be about vanity because it evokes that tradition is to miss the point. In fact, the longer I looked at the painting, the less its trappings mattered and the more I felt that I was looking at the enigmatic but unalterable fact of another person's life in a moment of sublime quiet and satisfaction. The mirror suggests Narcissus only to make it clear that he has no place here. The woman's gaze doesn't convey desire, but the end of desire: fulfillment.

Edward Snow, in *A Study of Vermeer* (University of California Press, 1979), reiterates throughout his essay that Vermeer's great paintings aren't moral but ontological. When I read his treatment of *The Procuress*, I was struck by how his reading corresponded to what I've always felt about that painting but had found hard to reconcile with its title. Snow argues that despite its vulgar subject, the painting, which has a woman as its radiant focus, conveys the peace of an erotic relationship so natural, so happy, that it defies moral analysis. In short, the woman of *The Procuress* isn't *bad*. All anyone has to do is look at her for a while to know that badness and goodness are not at issue here.

If every painting, particularly those of private life, makes the onlooker a voyeur, most of Vermeer's women undercut erotic voyeurism with their autonomy—very much in the way that the woman in *The Procuress* defies the leering onlooker in the painting itself, not by recognizing his leer but simply through the power of her being. It isn't that Vermeer's women are without eroticism—their physicality is undeniable—but rather that they resist definition as erotic objects. This fact is all the more marvelous in a painting in which the man has got his hand on the woman's breast. Even when Vermeer's women glance back at the viewer or look directly out of the painting, even when his subject is breathtakingly young and beautiful—as is the case in *Girl with a Pearl Earring*—she appears to be in full command of a separate and whole desire that is hers, not the spectator's. And although the subject of *Woman with a Pearl Necklace* invites voyeurism, it deflects it completely. Because she appears to be the object of her own gaze, what she is seeing repeats what the viewer of the painting sees, although from another angle. The mirror then would seem to be the narcissistic *end* of all this looking: "I love what I see." This is exactly what happens in the Frans van Mieris painting *Young Woman Before a Mirror*, where the dark frame of the mirror becomes the imaginary focus (because the woman's reflection isn't seen) of sensual desire for the self. But it doesn't happen in Vermeer's painting. And it doesn't happen because we know from the woman's face that what is being reflected there isn't self-love and, more important, because the entire far side of the canvas is opened up by the astonishing light that comes through the window.

While I was sitting on the bench in front of the painting, a word popped into my head. I didn't search for it. It just came. *Annunciation.* That bench was about six feet away from the painting, and from that distance the light of the pearls disappeared. They are softly illuminated with the most delicate dabs of paint, and I could see them very well when I was standing close to the picture; but from my bench I didn't see their light anymore, only the woman's hands raised in that quiet, mysterious gesture and the radiance of the window light, a light that no reproduction can adequately show. When I turned my head, almost as if to shake out the thought, I saw one of the exhibition's two curators, Arthur Wheelock, standing right beside me and remembered that "the press" had been told that either of them would be happy to answer any questions, and there he was, so I stood up and boldly asked: "Has anyone ever thought of this painting in terms of an Annunciation?" He looked a little funny at first. Then he shook his head and said, "No, but that's very interesting. I had thought of it as a Eucharistic gesture." And then, at the same time, we both lifted our hands as if to imitate the gesture of the woman with the pearls, which is itself an echo of the gesture from early Renaissance paintings in which Mary raises her hands toward the angel who comes to tell her that she is pregnant with God's son. Mr. Wheelock then thanked me a couple of times, which was very nice of him, and the simple fact that he didn't consider this idea an outrage gave me the confidence I needed to think it through. This thought, or maybe little epiphany, didn't leave me. I knew there were "Annunciations" buried in my brain that had been triggered by this Vermeer painting. Later, when I was reading through the catalog more carefully, I discovered that among the few things known about Vermeer's life is that he was summoned to the Hague in 1672 as an "expert in Italian paintings" (Wheelock, *Johannes Vermeer,* catalog, p. 16).

It is impossible to know what art Vermeer saw or what places he visited in Italy—if indeed he went to Italy at all. He converted to Catholicism before his marriage, and the painting of Saint Praxedis shows that, at least once, he painted a specifically Catholic subject, but no one knows whether it was a commissioned painting or not.[1] Nevertheless, Catholicism, with its many female saints and the central position of the Madonna, emphasizes women far more than Protestantism, and Vermeer's art suggests that, at the very least, this feminine side of his new faith must have appealed to him. Wheelock mentions the Eucharist in his catalog essay. Snow writes, "The woman appears not to be so much admiring the pearls in the mirror as selflessly, even reverently, offering them up to the light: it is as if we were present at a marriage." Two sacraments. Both thoughts are similar ways of explaining an experience of looking at something that feels holy. For Todorov, Vermeer's ascension is into art. The artist leaps beyond realism into the enchanted space of art itself, a leap that anticipates a much later aesthetic. All these readings are ways of explaining the magic—the secret that announces itself in the painting and doesn't go away. It may be that Vermeer's ambiguity allows all these readings, that this *is* what the painting *means*, and that, like all great art, it opens a space of possibility larger than what is circumscribed in lesser works.

Nevertheless, I am going to push my intuition further and suggest that the painting is also rife with an allusion to the Annunciation. After I had left Washington and returned to New York, I began mulling over the Annunciation problem and understood that the resemblance I had seen was not only gestural but spatial. On a hunch I turned first to Fra Angelico, who painted several Annunciations, and in his work from the San Marco frescoes in Florence I found an image as motionless as Vermeer's *Woman with a Pearl Necklace*. Intended for monastic meditation, the picture is stripped of all ornament and architectural detail. The event takes place in a bare gray cell. As was conventional, the Virgin is on the right as you face the painting, the angel on the left; but in this work there is nothing between them. The space is filled by a soft light that comes from the left, illuminating the back of the angel and the front of the Virgin. But the space is also filled by Mary's gaze. Her eyes, turned toward Gabriel, are the hypnotic focus of the work; and although her posture doesn't resemble Vermeer's woman, it must have been her eyes that my ruminations on *Woman with a Pearl Necklace* had called forth.

Nevertheless, there was a particular painting I had in mind, although its details had been lost to me, and in it was a Virgin with uplifted hands. I became convinced that I had seen the work in Sienna almost seventeen years ago and knew that I would recognize it if I came across it—and I did. It was a work by Duccio in

the Museo dell'Opera del Duomo in Sienna. That it was by
Duccio isn't strange. His Madonnas in the same museum are
among my favorite paintings in the world; and when I was there, I
spent a long time with them. Because Duccio inhabits that borderland between the icon and the human face of the Renaissance,
I have always found his figures achingly beautiful. In Vermeer, I
have seen something similar. The threshold is a later one, but in
Vermeer the sacred and the human are also joined, and the
memory of the icon lives in allegory—the form of allusion in
Dutch painting of the time.[2] But the Annunciation I remembered
by Duccio when I saw it reproduced was *The Annunciation of the
Death of the Virgin*. So, surely, if Vermeer knew his Italian art, he
would be making no specific reference to this work. After dig-
ging about, however, I discovered that the Virgin is shown with
uplifted hands in a number of Annunciation paintings, that this
posture does belong to the iconography of gesture in both Italian
and Flemish paintings of the period. Two examples to turn to are
one by Giusto de' Menabuoi (1367) and one by Dieric Bouts,
painted a hundred years later.[3]

At the recommendation of a friend, I turned to a book by
Michael Baxandall, *Painting and Experience in Fifteenth-Century Italy*
(Oxford University Press, 1972). Among other things, the author
discusses physical gesture in painting of the period, noting that
"the painter was a professional visualizer of holy stories" for a pub-
lic that through spiritual exercises was well versed in a similar
task—seeing in their minds events from the lives of Christ and
Mary. He cites a sermon by Fra Roberto Caracciolo da Lecce on
the Annunciation as an example of popular preaching on the
Immaculate Conception. In the sermon, Fra Roberto first discusses the "angelic mission." One of its categories is *time*: the
Annunciation took place on Friday, March 25, either in the morn-

ing or midday during the spring, when the earth was blooming after winter, an idea only broadly relevant to the Vermeer painting, in that it is obviously midday light that pours through the window. The "angelic colloquy," also discussed in the sermon, is a dissection into five stages of the biblical passage in Luke. Baxandall points to the colloquy as a guide to understanding the Virgin's gestures in paintings that depict the Annunciation at its various moments, from the first stage, *Conturbatio* (Disquiet) to the last, *Meritatio* (Merit). What Baxandall's discussion clarified for me was that although pictures of the Virgin were heavily coded, they weren't dictated by the church. Within that code there was significant range for the painter's own vision of how the Virgin's body would express Disquiet, for example. The painted images are a combination of convention, spiritual teaching, and imagination.

But it was the second stage of the colloquy that grabbed my attention: *Cogitatio* (Reflection). The Virgin receives the salutation of the angel and reflects on it. Knowing this places the mirror in *Woman with a Pearl Necklace* in a whole new context. Isn't that mirror, contiguous to the radiant window, a buried allusion to the Annunciation, and very likely to this second stage—Reflection?

Because I wanted to see more Annunciation paintings, I took a tour of the Metropolitan Museum, in New York, looking for them at random. I turned a corner and ran straight into the Petrus Christus painting of the event (a work that has also been attributed to Jan van Eyck) and was stopped in my tracks. I had seen it before but had never registered it deeply in my private catalog of remembered paintings. Although the Virgin's gesture is not like that of the woman with the pearls (she has one hand near her neck, clasping the folds of her cloak, while the other hand holds a book), I had discovered a Virgin whose posture is as erect and whose gaze is as clear and unflinching as Vermeer's woman. Between the Virgin and Gabriel is the Holy Spirit, depicted as a bird that gives off painted rays of light. The Virgin stands at the threshold of a door that divides the painting between inside and outside. The angel stands beyond the domestic interior. As I looked at this painting, it became even more apparent that my insight about the Annunciation—half unconscious as it was—rose out of not one, but many diffuse references in Vermeer's painting—that not only the woman's hands suggest the Annunciation, but so do the light from the window, her gaze, her posture, and that it is this accumulation of detail that produces the painting's feeling of quiet sanctity.

There is one further thing in *Woman with a Pearl Necklace* that confounded me from the instant I noticed it in the gallery. Above the window frame near the folds of the curtain is a small, egg-shaped detail. The truth is that when I first looked at it, I thought: What's that egg doing there? That "egg" is probably part of the window's architecture, and yet it appears to be almost distinct from it. In the museum, I went right up to it, but the closer I came to it, the harder it was to decipher. It appears as light and shadow itself or perhaps paint as light and shadow itself. But what's it doing there? We know that Vermeer changed the world he painted as he saw fit. Although he was interested in creating a *feeling* of realism, he changed objects, colors, shadows, even perspective at will to make what he wanted to make. Surely he wanted that oval "thing" on his window or he would have eliminated it. I started looking for that shape on other opened or shut windows in Vermeer's work, but couldn't find it. This round architectural detail contrasts with the linearity of the rest of the window. It echoes the shine of the woman's earring, the subtle gleam of her pearls, the roundness of the dark covered jar, the bowl, and the roundness of her own form—the flesh of her face and arms, all the while looking decidedly *egglike*. No wonder scholars have gone crazy "interpreting" Vermeer. There is allegorical allusion in his paintings, signs that can be read but that are also hidden inside ordinary rooms and in the faces of "real" people, and necessarily so, because these paintings are neither one thing nor the other. They are both.

Conception and pregnancy—that's what the Annunciation is about, after all—an explanation of the divine presence inside a human being. Natural pregnancy and its role in Dutch painting is an old dispute, and it pops up again with Vermeer, although not in regard to the woman with the pearls. Albert Blankert writes that van Gogh was the first person to suggest that the *Woman in Blue Reading a Letter* is pregnant and points out that the belly of Vermeer's virgin goddess Diana "looks thoroughly bulbous to twentieth century eyes" as well.[4] My personal response to this is that Diana doesn't look nearly as pregnant as the woman in blue, who appears to be on the brink of giving birth. No doubt the fashion of the day promoted the big belly as a sign of beauty, but this protruding belly must have been regarded as beautiful for the very reason that it mimicked pregnancy. When he died at forty-two, Vermeer left ten *minor* children. Obviously, pregnancies came and went at a rapid clip in his own household, and he must have had intimate knowledge of pregnancy in all its stages. Vermeer's attention to the physical detail of domestic life and to the women who inhabit it would necessarily have included the changing shape of women themselves. How could it not?

Neither her body nor her clothes tell us whether the woman with the necklace is pregnant. The hint of her pregnancy is in the

painting's relation to the Annunciation, to a miraculous beginning. It is in her gaze and in the luster of the pearls themselves,
which signify, among other things, purity and virginity. It is in her
unmoving fingers that call to mind the nearly uncanny quiet of
physical gesture in early Renaissance paintings—in which the
human body not only speaks for itself but also articulates
the codes of religious experience. The truth is, however, that the
whole painting conveys enclosure and privacy. The room, with its
closed window and single, egg-shaped detail, and the rotund covered jar in the foreground that blends with the vast piece of cloth,
are all lit by the enchanted light that comes from beyond the
room. We are allowed to look at a world sufficient unto itself,
a world that is lit by the holiness of an everyday miracle—
pregnancy and birth—perceived in the painting as a gift from
God, shining in God's light, which is also real light, the light of
day. The magic here is of being itself, never more fully experienced
than in pregnancy—two people in one body. Isn't this why the
woman communicates no desire—only completeness—and why
the light seems to hold her as much as the mirror?

Nevertheless, I want to emphasize that my reading is not
meant to reduce the painting to an Annunciation either. Vermeer
brought the miraculous into a room just like the rooms he knew,
and he endowed the features of an ordinary woman with spiritual
greatness. *Woman with a Pearl Necklace* is a painting that makes no
distinction between the physical and the spiritual world. Here
they are inseparable. Each merges within the other to form a
totality. In Vermeer, the gulf between the symbol and the real is
closed. *Woman with a Pearl Necklace* is a work of *reflection* at its
most sublime. The viewer reflects on the woman, who also reflects
and is reflected, and through this mirroring of wonder, Vermeer
elevates not only his creature—the woman in the painting—but

all of us who look at her—because looking at her and the memory of looking at her become nothing less than an affirmation of the strangeness and beauty of simply being alive.

NOTES

1. Arthur Wheelock, *Vermeer and the Art of Painting* (New Haven: Yale University Press, 1995), 22–24.

2. Tzvetan Todorov, *Éloge du Quotidien: Essai sur la peinture hollandaise de XVII siècle* (Paris: Société nouvelle Adam Biro, 1993), 43–53.

3. For these two examples, see reproductions of the *Annunciation* by Giusto de' Menabuoi (p. 48) and an *Annunciation* (by Dieric Bouts (p. 296), in *Giotto to Dürer: Early Renaissance Painting in the National Gallery*, by Jill Dunkerton, Susan Foister, Dillian Gordon, and Nicholas Penny (New Haven: Yale University Press, 1991).

4. Albert Blankert, *Catalogue Johannes Vermeer*, p. 39.

Gatsby's Glasses

I first read *The Great Gatsby* when I was sixteen years old, a high school student in Northfield, Minnesota. I read it again when I was twenty-three and living in New York City, and now again at the advanced age of forty-two. I have carried the book's magic around with me ever since that first reading, and its memory is distinct in my mind, because unlike many books that return to me chiefly as a series of images, *The Great Gatsby* has also left its trace in my ear—as enchanted music, whispering, laughter, and as the voice of storytelling itself.

The book begins with the narrator's memory of something his father told him years before: "Whenever you feel like criticizing anyone, remember that all the people in this world haven't had the advantages that you've had." As an adage for life, the quotation is anticlimactic—restrained words I imagine being uttered by a restrained man, perhaps over the top of his newspaper, and yet without this watered-down American version of noblesse oblige, there could be no story of Gatsby. The father's words are the story's seed, its origin. The man who we come to know as Nick

Carraway tells us that his father "meant a great deal more" than what the words denote, and I believe him. Hidden in the comment is a way of living and an entire moral world. Its resonance is double: first, we know that the narrator's words are bound to his father's words, that he comes from somewhere he can identify, and that he has not severed that connection; and second, that these paternal words have shaped him into who he is: a man "inclined to reserve all judgements"—in short, the ideal narrator, a man who doesn't leap into the action but stays on the sidelines. Nick is not an actor but a voyeur, and in every art, including the art of fiction, there's always somebody watching.

Taking little more than his father's advice, the young man goes east. The American story has changed direction: the frontier is flip-flopped from west to east, but the urge to leave home and seek your fortune is as old as fairy tales. Fitzgerald's Middle West was not the same as mine. I did not come from the stolid advantages of Summit Avenue in St. Paul. I remember those large, beautiful houses on that street as beacons of wealth and privilege to which I had no access. I grew up in the open spaces of southern Minnesota in one of the "lost Swede towns" Fitzgerald mentions late in the book, only we were mostly Norwegians, not Swedes. It was to my hometown that Fitzgerald sent Gatsby to college for two weeks. The unnamed town is Northfield. The named college is St. Olaf, where my father taught for thirty years and where I was a student for four. Gatsby's ghost may have haunted me, because even in high school, I knew that promise lay in the East, particularly in New York City, and ever so vaguely, I began to dream of what I had never seen and where I had never been.

Nick Carraway hops a train and finds himself in the bond trade and living next door to Gatsby's huge mansion: a house built of wishes. All wishes, however wrongheaded, however great or noble or ephemeral, must have an object, and that object is usually more ideal than real. The nature of Gatsby's wish is fully articulated in the book. Gatsby is *great*, because his dream is all-consuming and every bit of his strength and breath are in it. He is a creature of will, and the beauty of his will overreaches the tawdriness of his real object: Daisy. But the secret of the story is that there is no *great Gatsby* without Nick Carraway, only Gatsby, because Nick is the only one who is able to see the greatness of his wish.

Reading the book again, I was struck by the strangeness of a single sentence that seemed to glitter like a golden key to the story. It occurs when a dazed Gatsby finds his wish granted, and he is showing Daisy around the West Egg mansion. Nick is, as always, the third wheel. "I tried to go then," he says, "but they wouldn't hear of it; perhaps my presence made them feel more satisfactorily alone." The question is: In what way are two people more *satisfactorily* alone when somebody else is present? What on earth does this mean? I have always felt that there is a triangular quality to every love affair. There are two lovers and a third element—the idea of being in love itself. I wonder if it is possible to fall in love without this third presence, an imaginary witness to love as a thing of wonder, cast in the glow of our deepest stories about ourselves. It is as if Nick's eyes satisfy this third element, as if he embodies for the lovers the essential self-consciousness of love—a third-person account. When I read Charles Scribner III's introduction to my paperback edition, I was not at all surprised that an early draft of the novel was written by Fitzgerald in the third person. Lowering the narration into the voice of a character inside the story allows the writer to inhabit more fully the interstices of narrative itself.

The role of the onlooker is given quasi-supernatural status in the book in the form of the bespectacled eyes of T. J. Eckleburg, and it is to this faded billboard of an oculist in Queens that the grieving Wilson addresses his prayer: "You can't hide from God." When his friend tells him, "That's an advertisement," Wilson doesn't answer. The man needs an omniscient third person, and he finds it in Eckleburg, with his huge staring eyes. This speech occurs when Nick is not present, and yet the quality of the narration does not change. It is *as if* he were present. Nick's stand-in is a neighbor of Wilson's, Michaelis, who has presumably reported the scene to the narrator, but the reader isn't told this directly. Together, Michaelis and Nick Carraway form a complementary narration that finds transcendence in the image of Eckleburg's all-seeing, all-knowing eyes, a figure very like the third-person narrator of nineteenth-century novels who looks down on his creatures and their follies.

There is only one other noticeable pair of spectacles in the novel, those worn by "the owl-eyed man." One of Gatsby's hundreds of anonymous guests, he is first seen in the "Gothic library," a drunken fellow muttering excitedly that the books "are absolutely real." He had expected cardboard, he tells Nick and Jordan, and cannot get over his astonishment at the *reality* of these volumes. The owl-eyed man returns near the end of the book as Gatsby's only mourner besides the dead man's father and Nick. Like the image of Eckleburg, the owl-eyed man is both thoroughly mysterious and thoroughly banal. He tells Nick and Jordan that he's been drunk for a week and that he thought the books might help "sober" him up. Nameless, the man is associated exclusively with the library and his large glasses. Nick does not ask the owl-eyed man to attend the funeral. He has kept the day and place a secret to avoid gawkers and the press, but, out of nowhere, the man makes his appearance in the rain, and during that time he removes his glasses twice. The second time, he wipes them, "outside and in." I can see him doing it. For me the gesture is intimate, and although no handkerchief is mentioned, I see a white handkerchief, too, moving over the rain-spattered lenses. The cleaning of the glasses is ordinary and magical. The strange man is a second, specifically literary incarnation of Eckleburg, a witness to the problem of what's real and what isn't, a problem that is turned inside out through the idea of seeing through *special glasses*—the glasses of fiction.

The Great Gatsby is an oddly immaterial novel. In it there are only two characters with bodies that mean anything, bodies of vigor and appetite: Tom Buchanan and his mistress, Myrtle Wilson, whose alliance causes the book's tragedy. The rest of them, Gatsby, the hordes of guests, Jordan, and, above all, Daisy, seem to be curiously unanchored to the ground. They are pastel beings, beings of light and sound—creatures of the imagination. At Gatsby's parties, "men and girls" come and go "like moths," accompanied by an orchestra as if they were characters in a play or a movie. When Nick first sees Daisy and Jordan in East Egg, the girls are reclining on a huge sofa. "They were both in white, and their dresses were rippling and fluttering as if they had just been blown back in after a short flight around the room." They are as weightless as dollar bills, or maybe hundred dollar bills, blown up in a wind before they settle again to the ground, and whether or not Fitzgerald intended this lightness as another image of money in his novel, money is the source of the charm that envelops the ethereal creatures. Daisy's music is her own "thrilling" voice, and it sounds, as Gatsby says, "like money." But Nick is the one who elaborates on its timbre. In it he hears the jingle of coins and the rain of gold in fairy tales.

It may be that New York and its environs is the best place in the world to feel this particular bewitchment that all the pieties about honest poverty cannot disperse. Fitzgerald is right. Money in the Midwest may be respectable and it may even be considerable, but it is nothing like New York money. There was no money where I grew up, no "real" money, that is. The turkey farmers did well, and the dentists in town had a certain affluent shine to them, but, on the whole, status was measured in increments—a new *economy* car, unused skates, an automatic garage door–opener—and there was a feeling that it was wrong to have much more money than anybody else, and downright sinful to flaunt it if you had it. When I arrived in New York, the money I saw flabbergasted me. It sashayed on Fifth Avenue and giggled in galleries and generally showed itself off with such unabashed glee that it was impossible not to admire it or envy it, at least a little. And what I saw during my travels through the city in the early 1980s was no different from what Nick saw. Money casts a glow over things, a glow all the more powerful to people who haven't got it. No matter how clean or morally upright, poverty has cracks and corners of ugliness that nothing but money can close, and I remember the sense of relief and pleasure that would come over me when I sat in a good restaurant with white tablecloths and shining silver and flowers, and I knew that my date was a person who could afford to pay. And it happened during my lonely, impoverished student days that a man would lean across the table and invite me to an island or to another country or to a seaside resort, to an East Egg or a West Egg, and the truth was that the smell of money would waft over me, its scent like a torpor-inducing drug, and had there been no Middle West, no Northfield, Minnesota, no home with its strident Lutheran sanctions, no invisible parental eyes always watching me—in short: had I been somebody else, I might have been blown off to an Egg in a gust of wind and floated across the beach and out into the Sound to the strains of some foolish but melodic accompaniment.

Gravity is personal history. That is why Nick tells the reader about his family right away. The Carraways have been "prominent well-to-do people for three generations," three generations founded on the rock of a *hard*ware business, a business that trades in real *things*. In the East, Nick trades not in things, as his father does, but in paper, bonds that will generate more paper. Money that makes money. And money has built Gatsby's castle, a place as unreal as a theater set erected from bills or bonds or "cardboard," as the owl-eyed man suggests. It is a blur of excess and anonymity as vague as Gatsby's rumored past—a past we learn in bits and pieces but which is never whole—for he is a man interrupted, a man who has broken from his old life and his parents to become not somebody else so much as "Nobody"—a brilliant cipher. "Mr. Nobody from Nowhere" is Tom Buchanan's contemptuous expression. Gatsby's connections to others are tenuous or fabricated. He misrepresents himself to Daisy when he first meets her in Louisville, by implying that he comes from her world. Again the image of wind appears in Fitzgerald's prose. "As a matter of fact, he had no comfortable family standing behind him, and he was liable at the whim of an impersonal government to be blown anywhere about the world."

But in this ephemeral weightlessness of Gatsby's there is beauty, real beauty, and on this the whole story turns. The man's monstrous accumulation of *things* is nothing if not vulgar, a grotesque display as pitiful as it is absurd. But what Nick understands, as nobody else does, is that this mountain of things is the vehicle of a man's passion, and as objects they are nearly drained of material reality. The afternoon when Gatsby takes Daisy through his house, we are told that he "stares at his possessions in a dazed way, as though in her actual and astounding presence, none of it was any longer real." His nerves running high, the owner of the property begins pulling shirts from his closet, one gauzy, gorgeous article after another, "in coral and apple-green and lavender and faint orange, with monograms of Indian blue," piling them high before Nick and his beloved. Then Daisy bends her lovely head and weeps into the shirts. "It makes me sad because I've never seen such—such beautiful shirts before." I marveled again at the power of this passage, which is at once tender and ridiculous. But Fitzgerald lets neither feeling get the upper hand. Daisy pours out the grief of her young love for Gatsby into a heap of his splendid shirts without understanding her own feelings. But she recovers quickly. Sometime later the same afternoon, she stares out the window at pink clouds in a western sky and says to Gatsby, "I'd just like to get one of those pink clouds and put you in it and push you around." The shirts, the clouds, the dream are colored like a fading rainbow. Gatsby stands at the edge of his lawn and watches the green light across the water from Daisy's house. The last suit Nick sees him wearing is pink. If your feet are rooted to the ground, you can't be blown willy-nilly, but you can't fly up to those rosy clouds either. It's as simple as that.

Things and nothings. Bodies and nobodies. The ground and the air. The tangible and the intangible. The novel moves restlessly between these dichotomies. Surely Fitzgerald was right when he said that The Great Gatsby was "a new thinking out of the idea of illusion." Illusion is generally coupled with its opposite, reality, but where is the real? Is reality found in the tangible and illusion in the intangible? Besides the nuts and bolts of hardware out west, there is *ground* in the novel, the soil of ashes in West Egg, the ground that Eckleburg unblinkingly surveys, but it is here that Fitzgerald lavishes a prose that could have been taken straight from Dickens, a prose of fantasy, not realism.

> This is the valley of ashes—a fantastic farm where ashes grow like wheat into ridges and hills and grotesque gardens; where ashes take the forms of houses and chimneys and rising smoke, and finally, with a transcendent effort, of men who move dimly and already crumbling through the powdery air.

With its crumbling men, the valley of ashes plainly evokes that other biblical valley of death, and this miserable stretch of land borders the road where Myrtle Wilson will die under the wheels of the car driven by Daisy. But like the pink clouds, it lacks solidity and dissolves. The difference between the vision of Gatsby's mansion and this earth is that money does not disguise mortality here. The gaping cracks of poverty are fully visible.

Nevertheless, among the residents of this ashen valley is Myrtle Wilson, the only person in the novel to whom Fitzgerald assigns "vitality." The word is used three times in reference to Mrs. Wilson, Tom Buchanan's working-class mistress: ". . . there was an immediately perceptible *vitality* about her as if the nerves of her body were continually smouldering." As Nick passes Wilson's gas station in a car, he sees her "at the garage pump with panting *vitality*." And in death: "The mouth was wide open and ripped at the corners, as though she had choked a little in giving up the tremendous *vitality* she had stored so long." It is this vivid life, not her character, that makes Myrtle Wilson's death tragic. A silly and coarse woman, she is nevertheless more sympathetic than her lover, Tom, who is worse: stupid and violent. Between them, however, there exists a real sexual energy that isn't found elsewhere in the novel. The narrator's attraction to Jordan is tepid at best, and Gatsby's fantasies about Daisy seem curiously unerotic. The slender girl has no body to speak of. She seems to be made of her beautiful clothes and her beautiful voice. It is hard to imagine Gatsby actually having sex with Daisy. It's like trying to imagine a man taking a butterfly. And although her marriage to Tom has produced a daughter, as a mother Daisy communicates detachment. She coos endearments at the child, Pammy, and then dismisses her. Only once in the novel is the reader reminded of Daisy as a creature of flesh and blood, and, significantly, it is through a finger her husband has bruised. Daisy looks down at the little finger "with an awed expression." "You didn't mean to," she says to Tom, "but you *did* do it." The passage is not only a premonition of Tom's brutality that erupts horribly in New York when he breaks Myrtle's nose or of Myrtle's bruised and opened body on the road. Daisy's awe expresses her remote relation to her own body and to mortality itself, which her money will successfully hide, not forever, of course, but for now.

What Tom and Myrtle have that Jay and Daisy don't is a *personal* relation, with its attendant physicality and mess. That is why, after admitting to Nick that Daisy may have once loved Tom "for a minute," Gatsby comforts himself by saying, "In any case, it was only personal." What Gatsby has been chasing all these years is neither *personal* nor *physical*. Its transcendence may have been lodged in the person of Daisy, but it is not limited to her. Her very shallowness makes Gatsby's dream possible. But Myrtle Wilson is not a simple incarnation of the flesh and its weaknesses. She harbors dreams as well. As it does for Gatsby, her intangible wish finds form in an object. In her drawer at home, wrapped in tissue paper, Mr. Wilson finds the expensive dog leash Tom once bought for her to go with the dog he also bought. The dog didn't come home. The useless, beautiful thing is a sign of absence, a string of absences, in fact—the dog, the lover, and the emptiness of desire itself. Just as the green light shining from Daisy's house may be counted among Gatsby's "enchanted objects," one he loses when Daisy actually enters his life again, the dog leash possesses a kind of magic. It is the tissue paper that makes me want to cry, that sends this frivolous possession into another register altogether, that imbues the silver-and-leather dog leash with the quality of true pathos.

The tangible and the intangible collide to cast a spell. But can a person or thing ever be stripped naked? Can we ever discover reality hiding under the meanings we give to people and things? I don't think so. And I don't think Fitzgerald thought so either. His book meditates on the necessity of fiction, not only as lies but as truths. The play between the material and the immaterial in *The Great Gatsby* is riddled, not simple. The fairy tale contains the valley of ashes as well as the castle by the sea, the heavy weight of the corpse and the pretty bodies blown in the wind. And which one is more real than the other? Is death more true than life? Are not dreams as much a part of living as waking life is? The book goes to the heart of the problem of fiction itself by insisting that fiction is necessary to life—not only as books but as dreams, dreams that frame the world and give it meaning. Nick imagines Gatsby at the pool just before Wilson kills him. The man has understood that there will be no message from Daisy, that the great idea is dead.

> He must have looked up at an unfamiliar sky through frightening leaves and shivered as he found what a grotesque thing a rose is and how raw the sunlight was upon the scarcely created grass. A

new world, material without being real, where poor ghosts, breathing dreams like air, drifted fortuitously about . . . like that ashen, fantastic figure gliding toward him through the amorphous trees.

This passage tells of dramatic change, but it is not a change from illusion to reality, from enchanted nature to real nature. This world may be new, but there are ghosts here, and they are fantastic. It is now a world made of matter, but that matter is no more real than the magic lights and music of the summer parties that went before it.

One can argue that nearly every word of dialogue uttered in the novel, every exchange, and every event is ordinary. Tom Buchanan and the poor Wilsons are glaringly limited and unattractive. Gatsby's business partner, Wolfsheim, is clever and dishonest without the grandeur of being satanic. Daisy's charm is not revealed in anything she says. Gatsby converses in a stiff and clichéd manner that sets Nick back on his heels. Jordan is a cheat. These characters do not elevate themselves above the crowd. They are not remarkable people, and yet to read this novel is to feel as if you have taken a walk in a fairy wood, as if while you are reading, you glimpse the sublime.

The magic is in the book's narration, in its shades of sunlight and darkness, its allusions to fairy tales, to music, songs, to dusty dance slippers and bright voices. Better than any other writer I know, Fitzgerald captures the tipsy aura of parties, that slight glazing of the mind that dawns after two glasses of champagne. The ordinary world trembles with *adjectival* enchantment here— Fitzgerald's prose is dense with surprising adjectives. Although some of his characters are glib, the narrator is not. The sorcery that infuses the book cannot be explained as the golden effect of money, although that is part of it, or even by youth. They are mostly very young, these people, and life still holds an unwrapped newness for them. Nick Carraway's voice carries a deeper understanding of enchantment, which at once grounds and elevates the narration. It returns us to the beginning. The father's words render up a world in which every human being, no matter how flawed, is granted an essential dignity. Remember, every person is a product of his own history, one that is not necessarily like yours. He or she has come out of a particular story and to judge that man or woman is not fair unless you know the story. The advice is a call to empathy, the ultimate act of the imagination, and the true ground of all fiction. All characters are born of this effort to be another person. And its success is rooted in the grounded self. The "carelessness" of Tom and Daisy manifests itself in flightiness. Unballasted, they flit from one place to another, and their wealth only facilitates their disconnectedness. Yet we trust Nick, this man who speaks to us, and we believe him when he says, "I am one of the few honest people that I have ever known." And we trust his *imaginings*, because the imaginary is crucial to his tale. He did not witness Gatsby's murder. He cannot be Gatsby, but he says, "He must have . . ." Nick Carraway's voice bears the conviction of his empathy.

Fitzgerald did not give part of Nick's story to Michaelis because it was convenient. By seamlessly transferring Nick's vision into Wilson's Greek neighbor, Fitzgerald lifts the narration out of the "merely personal." Nick sees beyond himself, and this second sight is reinforced by the eyes of Eckleburg and the owl eyes of the man in the library. Nick sees vicariously what Michaelis and another man actually witness: Myrtle's dead body, the body Daisy will not see and cannot face. It is more than enough. The men undo Mrs. Wilson's shirt "still wet with perspiration" and see "that her left breast was hanging loose like a flap, and there was no need to listen to the heart below." Later Nick tells Gatsby, "She was ripped open." He did not have to be there to see. For a moment, with Nick, the reader stares into the heart of being, and it has stopped. I see what I did not see. I experience that which is outside my own experience. This is the magic of reading novels. This is the working out of the problem of illusion. I take a book off the shelf. I open it up and begin to read, and what I discover in its pages is real.

A Plea for Eros

A few years ago a friend of mine gave a lecture at Berkeley on the *femme fatale*, a subject he has been thinking about for years. When I met him, he was a graduate student at Columbia University, but now he is a full-fledged philosopher, and when it is finished, his book will be published by Gallimard in France and Harvard University Press in America. He is Belgian but lives in Paris, a detail significant to the story, because he comes from another rhetorical tradition—a French one. When he finished speaking, he took questions, including a hostile one from a woman who demanded to know what he thought of the Antioch Ruling—a law enacted at Antioch College, which essentially made every stage of a sexual encounter on campus legal only by verbal consent. My friend paused, smiled, and replied: "It's wonderful. I love it. Just think of the erotic possibilities: 'May I touch your right breast? May I touch your left breast?' " The woman had nothing to say.

This little exchange has lingered in my mind. What interests me is that he and she were addressing exactly the same problem, the idea of permission, and yet their perspectives were so far apart that it was as if they were speaking different languages. The woman expected opposition, and when she didn't get it, she was speechless. Aggressive questions are usually pedagogic—that is, the answer has already been written in the mind of the questioner, who then waits with a reply. It's pretend listening. But by moving the story—in this case, the narrative of potential lovers—onto new ground, the young philosopher tripped up his opponent.

It is safe to assume that the Antioch Ruling wasn't devised to increase sexual pleasure on campus, and yet the new barriers it made, ones which dissect both sexual gestures and the female body (the ruling came about to protect women, not men), have been the stuff of erotic fantasy for ages. When the troubadour pined for his lady, he hoped against hope that he would be granted a special favor—a kiss perhaps. The sonnet itself is a form that takes the body of the beloved apart—her hair, her eyes, her lips, her breasts. The body in pieces is reborn in this legal drama of spoken permission. Eroticism thrives both on borders and on distance. It is a commonplace that sexual pleasure demands thresholds. My philosopher made quick work of demonstrating the excitement of crossing into forbidden territory—the place you need special permission to trespass into. But there is distance here, too, a distance the earnest crusaders who invented the ruling couldn't possibly have foreseen. The articulation of the other's body in words turns it into a map of possible pleasure, effectively distancing that body by transforming it into an erotic object.

Objectification has a bad name in our culture. Cries of "Women are not sexual objects" have been resounding for years. I first ran into this argument in a volume I bought in the ninth grade called *Sisterhood Is Powerful*. I carried that book around with me until it fell apart. Feminism was good for me, as were any number of causes, but as I developed as a thinking person, the truisms and dogmas of every ideology became as worn as that book's cover. Of course women are sexual objects; so are men. Even while I was hugging that book of feminist rhetoric to my chest, I groomed myself carefully, zipped myself into tight jeans, and went after the boy I wanted most, mentally picking apart desirable male bodies like a connoisseur. Erotic pleasure, derived from the most intimate physical contact, thrives on the paradox that only by keeping alive the strangeness of that other person can eroticism last. Every person is keenly aware of the fact that sexual feeling is distinct from affection, even though they often conspire, but this fact runs against the grain of classic feminist arguments.

American feminism has always had a puritanical strain, an imposed blindness to erotic truth. There is a hard, pragmatic aspect to this. It is impolitic to admit that sexual pleasure comes in all shapes and sizes, that women, like men, are often aroused by what seems silly at best and perverse at worst. And because sexual excitement always partakes of the culture itself, finds its images and triggers from the boundaries delineated in a given society, the whole subject is a messy business.

Several years ago I read an article in *The New York Times* about a Chinese version of the Kinsey Report, the results of which suggested that Chinese women as a group experienced *no* sexual pleasure. This struck me as insane, but as I began to ponder the idea, it took on a kind of sense. I visited China in 1986 to find a place still reeling from the Cultural Revolution, a place in which pre-revolutionary forms appeared to have been utterly forgotten. Maybe there can't be much erotic life, other than the barest minimum, without an encouraging culture—without movies and books, without ideas about what it's supposed to be. When I was fifteen, I remember watching *Carnal Knowledge* at the Grand movie theater in Northfield, Minnesota, my hometown. Jack Nicholson and Ann-Margret were locked in a mystifying upright embrace and were crashing around the room with their clothes on, or most of them on, banging into walls and making a lot of noise, and I had absolutely no idea what they were doing. It had never occurred to me in my virginal state that people made love *like that*. A friend had to tell me what I was seeing. Most teenagers today are more sophisticated, but only because they've had more exposure. I was thirteen before I stumbled over the word *rape*—in *Gone with the Wind*. I walked downstairs and asked my mother what it meant. She looked at me and said, "I was afraid of that." Then she told me. But even after I knew, I didn't really understand it, and I couldn't imagine it.

My point is this: a part of me has real sympathy for the Chinese couple, both university professors, who married, went to bed with each other faithfully every night, and, after a year, visited a doctor, wondering why no child had come from their union. They thought sleeping *beside* each other was enough. Nobody told them that more elaborate activity was necessary. Surely this is a case of an erotic culture gone with the wind. (In China among the class that could afford to cultivate it, the female body had become a refined sexual art form. In Xi'an I saw a very old woman with bound feet. She could no longer walk and had to be carried. Those tiny, crippled feet were the gruesome legacy of a lost art. Binding feet made them small enough to fit into a man's mouth.) The famous parental lecture on the birds and the bees, the butt of endless jokes and deemed largely unnecessary in our world, never took place in the lives of the two puzzled professors. *But where were their bodies?* We imagine that proximity would be enough, that *natural* forces would lead the conjugal couple to sexual happiness. But my feeling is that it isn't true, that all of us need a story outside ourselves, a form through which we imagine ourselves as players in the game.

Consider standard erotic images. Garter belts and stockings, for example, still have a hold on the paraphernalia of arousal— even though, except for the purpose of titillation, they have mostly vanished from women's wardrobes. Would these garments be sexy if you'd never seen them before? Would they mean anything? But we can't escape the erotic vocabulary of our culture any more than we can escape language itself. There's the rub. Although feminist discourse in America understandably wants to subvert cultural forms that aren't "good" for women, it has never taken on the problem of arousal with much courage. When a culture oppresses women, and all do to one degree or another, it isn't convenient to acknowledge that there are women who like submission in bed or who have fantasies about rape. Masochistic fantasies damage the case for equality, and even when they are seen as the result of a "sick society," the peculiarity of our sexual actions or fantasies is not easily untangled or explained away. The ground from which they spring is simply too muddy. Acts can be controlled, but not desire. Sexual feeling pops up, in spite of our politics.

Desire is always between a subject and an object. People may have loose, roving appetites, but desire must fix on an object even if that object is imaginary, or narcissistic—even if the self is turned into an other. Between two real people, the sticky part is beginning. As my husband says, "Somebody has to make the first move." And this is a delicate matter. It means reading another person's desires. But misreading happens, too. When I was in my early twenties in graduate school, I met a brilliant, astoundingly articulate student with whom I talked and had coffee. I was in love at the time with someone else, and I was unhappy, but not unhappy enough to end the relation. This articulate student and I began going to the movies, sharing Chinese dinners, and talking our heads off. I gave him poems of mine to read. We talked about books and more books and became *friends* (as the saying goes). I was not attracted to him sexually at all, nor did I glean any sexual interest in me from him. He didn't flirt. He didn't make any moves, but after several months, our friendship blew up in my face. It became clear that he had pined and suffered, and that I had been insensitive. The final insult to him turned on my having given him a poem to criticize that had as its subject the sexual power of my difficult boyfriend. I felt bad. Perhaps never in my life have I so misinterpreted a relation with another person. I have always prided myself on having a nearly uncanny ability to receive unspoken messages, to sense underlying intentions, even unconscious ones, and here I had bollixed up the whole business. No doubt we were both to blame. He was too subtle, and I was distracted—fixated on another body. Would the Antioch Ruling have helped us? I doubt it. A person who doesn't reach out for your hand or stroke your face or come near you for a kiss isn't about to propose these overtures out loud. He was a person without any coarseness of mind, much too refined to leap. He thought that dinner and the movies meant that we were on a "date," that he had indicated his interest through the form of our evenings. I, on the other hand, had had lots of dinners and movies with fellow students, both men and women, and it didn't occur to me that the form signified anything in particular; and yet the truth was, I should have known. Because he was so discreet, and because I lacked all sexual feeling for him, I assumed he had none for me.

Nineteenth-century conventions for courtship have been largely disassembled in the latter half of this century, bending the codes out of shape. People marry later. The emphasis on virginity for women has changed. Single women work and are not expected to give up their jobs once they marry. Men have been digesting a set of new rules that are nevertheless colored by the old ones. People still court each other, after all. They are still looking for Romance of one kind or another—short or long—and each one of them is alone out there reading and misreading the intentions of others. The Antioch Ruling was clearly a response to the chaos of courtship—a way of imposing a structure on what seemed to have collapsed—but ambiguity remains, not just in interpretation but even in desire itself. There are people, and we have all met them, who can't make up their minds. There are people who say no when they mean yes, and yes when they mean no. There are people who mean exactly what they say when they say it, and then later wish they had said the opposite. There are people who succumb to sexual pressure out of a misplaced desire to please or even out of pity. To pretend ambiguity doesn't exist in sexual relations is just plain stupid.

And then there are moments of interruption—those walls that block desire. I was absolutely mad about a boy in high school, but there was something about his nose when he kissed me, something about its apparent softness from that angle that I disliked. To my mind, that nose needed more cartilage. I kept my eyes shut. I know of a woman who fell for a man at a party. She fell hard and fast. They returned to her apartment in an erotic fever, kissing madly, throwing their clothes off, and then she looked across the room and saw his underwear. If I remember correctly, it was some male version of the bikini bottom, and her attraction vanished suddenly, irrevocably. She told the poor man to leave. An explanation was impossible. What was she to say? I hate your underpants?

Sexual freedom and eroticism are not identical; in fact, freedom can undermine the erotic, because the no-holds-barred approach is exciting only if you've just knocked down the door. And despite the fact that dinner, a movie, and a kiss at the door have taken a beating in recent years, seduction is inevitably a theater of barriers, a playing and replaying of roles, both conscious and unconscious. Sincerity is not at issue here; most of us play in earnest. Through the language of clothes and gesture and through talk itself, we imagine ourselves as the other person will see us, mirroring our own desire in them, and most of what we do is borrowed from a vocabulary of familiar images. This is not a territory of experience that is easy to dissect legally.

Apparently, there is a new law in Minnesota against staring. It has been duly mocked in newspapers all over the world, but according to my sister, it came about because of the increase in the number of construction sites around Minneapolis, and women were weary of walking past them. Most women have experienced these painful, often humiliating excursions in front of an ogling, jeering crowd of men, and I don't know of anybody who likes them. This event—the construction crew whooping and hooting at a passing woman—is a convention, a thing those guys do in a group and only in a group, to liven up the job, to declare their masculinity to the world *safely*. It's the pseudo-sexual invitation. Not a single one of those men expects the woman to say, "Yes, I'm flattered. Take me, now."

But staring, even staring in this crude form, does not seem criminal to me. "Officer, he's staring. Arrest him," has a feeble ring to it. And I say this despite the fact that twice in my life I found myself the object of what would have to be described as aggressive staring. For several years, when I was in high school and then attending college in the same town, a young man I knew only slightly would appear out of nowhere and stare. He did not stare casually. He stared wholeheartedly and with such determination, he made me nervous and uncomfortable, as if he did it to satisfy some deep longing inside him. Without any warning, I would find him stationed outside the restaurant where I worked or outside the student union at my college, his eyes fixed on me. They were enormous pale eyes, ringed with black, that made him look as if he hadn't slept in weeks. "I've been standing here since eight o'clock this morning," he said to me once at three in the afternoon, "waiting for you." One night after work he followed me through the streets. I panicked and began to run. He did not pursue me. The problem was that he acted in ways that struck me as unaccountable. He would make abrupt changes in his appearance—suddenly shaving his head, for example. He walked all the way to my parents' house to deliver a gift, badly packed in a cardboard box. Filled with dread, I opened the box, only to find an ugly but innocent green vase. Not long before I received the vase, this young man's twin brother had killed himself in a cafe in a nearby town. He had gone there for breakfast and then after finishing his meal, took out a gun and blew his brains out. I am sure I associated the actions of the twin with the one who survived, am sure that the staring frightened me because I imagined potential violence lurking behind those eyes. The looks he gave me were beyond anything I had ever encountered, but I also honestly believe he meant me no harm. Perhaps in his own way he was in love. I don't know. But the crux of the story is that I think I brought it on myself without meaning to. Once, when I was in high school, I hugged him.

I worked at a place called the Youth Emergency Service, and the staring boy used to hang out there. I don't know where he lived or how he managed. He didn't go to school. He was sad that day, as he probably was most days, and we talked. I have no recollection of that conversation, but I know that in a fit of compassion, I hugged him. I am convinced that the whole staring problem hinged on this hug, and to this day when I think of it, I am mortified. Acts cannot be retrieved and, sometimes, they last. This is not a simple story. I often wonder if any story is, if you really look at it, but I carry his face around with me and when I think of him and the former me, I feel sorry for both of us.

The other staring man was a student of mine at Queens College. I taught freshman English there and an introductory literature class. My teaching was passionate, occasionally histrionic, but I was a young woman on a mission to educate, and sometimes I did. This student was clearly intelligent, although he had profound and jarring diction problems. His papers were written in a gnarled, convoluted style that was meant to be elevated but was often merely wrong. Eventually, I came to recognize that there had been signs of schizophrenia in the writing, but that wasn't until later. I had private sessions with all my students. These meetings were required, and when I met with him, I urged simplicity and hiding his thesaurus forever. The trouble began when he was no longer my student. He would barge into my office unannounced and throw unwanted gifts onto my desk—records, perfume, magazines. He, too, had a penchant for inexplicable transformations, for flannel shirts one day and silky feminine tops the next. On a balmy afternoon in late April, he visited me wearing a fur coat. Another time, I looked up to find him standing in my little graduate-assistant cubicle, his fingers busily unbuttoning his shirt.

This story rings with comedy now, but I was aghast. In my best schoolteacher voice, I shouted, "Stop!" He looked terribly hurt and began stamping his foot like a three-year-old, whining my *first* name, as though he couldn't believe I had thwarted him. After that, he would park himself outside the classroom where I taught and stare at me. If I looked a little to the right, I would see him in my peripheral vision. The staring unnerved me, and after several days of it, I was scared. When I crossed campus, he would follow me—an omnipresent ghost I couldn't shake. Talking to him did no good. Yelling at him did no good. I went to the campus police. They were indifferent to my alarm. No, more than that, they were contemptuous. I had no recourse. In time, the student gave up, and my ghost disappeared, never to bother me again. The question is, What does this story exemplify? Would it be called sexual harassment now, because of that shirt episode? Is it stalking? What he actually *did* to me was innocuous. The fear came from the fact that what he did was unpredictable. He did not play by the rules, and once those rules had been broken, I imagined that anything was possible.

Neither of these staring experiences was erotic for me, but they may have been for the two young men who did the staring. Who I was for either of them remains a mystery to me, a blank filled with my own dread. They have lasted inside me as human signs of the mysteries of passion, of emotional disturbance and tumult, and despite the unpleasantness they caused me, I am not without compassion for both of them. I have stared myself. Looking hard is the first sign of eros, and once when I was fourteen, I found myself staring very hard at a house. I had fallen in love with a boy who was fifteen. He cared nothing for me and was involved with a girl who had what I didn't have: breasts. She fascinated me almost as much as he did, because, after all, she was his beloved, and I studied her carefully for clues to her success. One Saturday in the fall, I walked to his house, stood outside on the sidewalk, and stared at it for a long time. I'm not sure why I did this. Perhaps I hoped he would walk out the door, or maybe I thought I might gain the courage to ring the bell. I remember that the house looked deserted. Probably no one was home. It was a corner house on a beautiful street in Northfield, lined with elms. The elms are all dead now, but I remember the street with trees. That house, which once was his house, is still suffused with the memory of my terrible ache for him, a longing I found almost unbearable and which was never requited. Years later, when I was grown (much taller than he ever grew) and I saw him in a local bar, he remembered my "crush" and said he regretted not acting on it. As silly as it sounds, this confession of his gave me real satisfaction, but the fact is he didn't want the fourteen-year-old I had been, but the twenty-two-year-old I had become—another person altogether.

Ogling should be legal. Looking is part of love, but what you see when you look is anybody's guess. Why that skinny ninth-grade boy with glasses sent me into paroxysms of longing, I couldn't tell you, but he did. Feelings are crude. The ache of love feels remarkably like the ache of grief or guilt. Emotional pain isn't distinguishable by feeling, only by language. We give a name to the misery, not because we recognize the feeling but because we know its context. Sometimes we feel bad and don't know why or don't remember why. Mercifully, love is sometimes equal, and two people, undisturbed by the wrong underwear or the wrong nose, find each other inside this mystery of attraction and are happy. But why?

Contentment in love usually goes unquestioned. Still, I don't think enduring love is rational any more than momentary flings. I have been married to the same man for fifteen years, and I can't explain why he still attracts me as an erotic object. He does, but why? Shouldn't it all be worn out by now? It is *not* because we are so close or know each other so well. That solidifies our friendship, not our attraction. The attraction remains because there's something about him that I can't reach, something strange and estranging. I like seeing him from a distance. I know that. I like to see him in a room full of people when he looks like a stranger, and then to remember that I do know him and that I will go home with him. But why he sometimes strikes me as a magical being, a person unlike others, I can't tell you. He has many good features, but so do other men that leave me cold as a stone. Have I given him this quality because it is efficient for me, or is it actually in him, some piece of him that I will never conquer and never know? It must be both. It must be between us—an enchanted space that is wholly unreasonable and, at least in part, imaginary. There is still a fence for me to cross and, on the other side of it, a secret.

Love affairs and marriages stand or fall on this secret. Familiarity and the pedestrian realities of everyday life are the enemies of eros. Emma Bovary watches her husband eat and is disgusted. She studies maps of Paris and hopes for something grander, more passionate, unfamiliar. A friend of mine told me about evenings out with her husband, during which they seduce each other all over again, and she can't wait to get home and jump on his beautiful body; but if on the way into the house he pauses to straighten the lids on the garbage cans, the spell is broken. She told him, and he now resists this urge. These interruptions disturb the stories we tell ourselves, the ready-made narratives that we have made our own. A combination of biology, personal history, and a cultural miasma of ideas creates attraction. The fantasy lover is always hovering above or behind or in front of the real lover, and you need both of them. The problem is that the alliance of these two is unpredictable. Eros, after all, was a mischievous little imp with arrows, a fellow of surprises who delighted in striking those who expected it least. Like his fairy reincarnation, Puck in *A Midsummer Night's Dream*, he makes madness of reason. He turns the world upside down. Hermia prefers Lysander to Demetrius for no good reason. Shakespeare's young men, Demetrius and Lysander, as has often been pointed out, are as alike and interchangeable as two pears. When Theseus points out to Hermia that Demetrius is just as good as Lysander, he isn't lying. It's just that Demetrius is not the one she likes. After much confusion and silliness, the lovers are set right by magic. Demetrius is never disenchanted. The flower juice remains in his eyes and he marries Helena under its influence, the point being that when we fall in love, we've all got fairy juice in our eyes, and not one of us gives a jot about the sane advice of parents or friends or governments.

And that's why legislating desire is unwieldy. A child rushes over and kisses another child in school in New York City, and he's nabbed by the authorities for "sexual harassment." Maybe it was an aggressive act, a sudden lack of control that needed the teacher's attention. Maybe the kissed child was unhappy or scared. And maybe, contrary to the myth of childish innocence, it was *sexual*, a burst of strange, wild feeling. I don't know. But people, children and adults, do bump up against each other. Everywhere, all the time there are scuffles of desire. We have laws against molestation and rape. Using power and position to extract sexual favors from an unwilling employee is ugly and shouldn't be legal. But on the other side of these crimes is a blurry terrain, a borderland of dreams and wishes. And it isn't a landscape of sunshine only. It is a place streaked with the clouds of sadism and masochism, where peculiar objects and garments are strewn here and there, and where its inhabitants weep as often as they sigh with pleasure. And it is nothing less than amazing that we should have to be reminded of this. All around us, popular singers are crooning out their passion and bitterness on the radio. Billboards, advertisements, and television shows are playing to our erotic weaknesses twenty-four hours a day. But at the same time, there is a kind of spotty cultural amnesia in particular circles, a block-headed impulse to crush complexity and truth in the name of right-thinking.

Once when I was attending a panel discussion on the fate or the state of "the novel," at the 92nd Street Y, because my husband had been roped into moderating this discussion, I listened to a novelist, an intelligent and good writer, berate Kafka for his depic-tions of women. They were bad, she said, wrongheaded. But in Kafka's world of dreams and claustrophobia, a world of irre-ducible images so powerful they shake me every time I remember them, what does it mean to second-guess its genius, to edit out the women who lift their skirts for the wandering K? When I read Kafka, I am not that housemaid who presents herself to the tor-mented hero anyway. I am the hero, the one who takes the plea-sure offered, as we all do when we sleep.

This is my call for eros, a plea that we not forget ambiguity and mystery, that in matters of the heart, we acknowledge an abiding uncertainty. I honestly think that when we are possessed by erotic magic, we don't feel like censoring Kafka or much else, because we are living a story of exciting thresholds and irrational feel-ing. We are living in a secret place we make between us, a place where the real and unreal commingle. That's where the young philosopher took the woman with the belligerent question. He brought her into a realm of the imagination and of memory, where lovers are alone speaking to each other, saying yes or no or "perhaps tomorrow," where they play at who they are, inventing and reinventing themselves as subjects and objects; and when the woman with the question found herself there, she was silent. Maybe, just maybe, she was remembering a passionate story of her own.

O.M.F. *Revisited*

1 *Metaphor*

The act of reading still surprises me, especially reading novels. The fact that I can look down at little symbols on a page and translate them into images and voices continues to astonish me. When I remember books, I don't remember the words on the page. I remember what I saw and heard the way I remember the real world. Sometimes when I go back to a book, I realize that I remembered wrong. And yet, every reading is an encounter with words, nothing more and nothing less. Over the years, I have read many books. Some of them have vanished. Others have lingered in my mind and changed me forever. One of them is the last novel Charles Dickens finished, *Our Mutual Friend*. It is a book about the world's secrets, about what we know and what we can't know, about what is spoken and what is unspoken. In it I found not answers but ultimate questions. More than any other writer I have read, Dickens is close to the metaphysical strangeness of things, to living and dying, and to the desire to put all of it into words.

The novel begins at twilight. The narrator looks over the dark water of the Thames and notices a boat, but it's hard to see in the bad light. Through the magic of omniscience, he moves closer. The boat has "no inscription," no identifying marks whatsoever. It is nameless. In it we see a man and a girl. Suddenly a slant of light from the waning sun illuminates the craft's bottom, "touching a rotten stain there which bore some resemblance to the outline of a muffled human form." The secret of the book is here. The stain will generate a world of muffled human forms, because this is a story of bodies, both dead and alive, and the marks they leave on the world, and it is a story of recognition and identification, which turns out to be a very murky business indeed.

The plot in a nutshell is this: The rotting body that left its stain in the boat is soon discovered, and the papers found on it lead the authorities to identify it as John Harmon, son of a London dust mogul and heir to a fortune. But the officials are wrong, and this case of mistaken identity will turn the world of the book upside down. The Boffins, loyal servants to old Harmon, become heirs to the fortune. Silas Wegg, a sly observer of the Boffins' new wealth, plots against them. A cash award, offered for information leading to the perpetrator of the murder, inspires Riderhood, a low-life river rat, to a deception that takes him to the offices of Eugene Wrayburn and Mortimer Lightwood, lawyers for the Harmon estate. Riderhood then accuses Gaffer Hexam, the man in the boat who found the body, of murder. This, in turn, brings the highborn Eugene Wrayburn and the lowborn Lizzie Hexam together, and their love story begins. Most important, the false identification of the body allows the real John Harmon, who has been away from home for many years, to pose as someone else, to become a spectator of his own death. He goes to live in what was once his father's house, where he works as a secretary to Boffin and observes the beautiful but spoiled Bella Wilfer, ward to the newly flush servants and the woman to whom he has been given in his father's will—his marriage to her being a condition of his inheritance. Another rocky courtship begins. Through social connection or simple coincidence, all the dispersed elements of the story intersect or collide: Lizzie and Bella meet. Bradley Headstone, schoolmaster to Lizzie's brother, and Eugene Wrayburn are thrown together and become rivals for Lizzie, and in the grip of what proves to be a fatal libidinous passion for Lizzie, Headstone allies himself with Riderhood. *Our Mutual Friend* is a story of love, money, greed, and dying—usually by drowning.

At one time or another, almost all the book's male characters end up dead or almost dead in the river. The cadaver dredged from the river slime turns out to be George Radfoot. When Radfoot is killed, Harmon, too, nearly drowns. Gaffer Hexam eventually drowns as he goes about his business of robbing the bloated bodies he dredges up from the Thames. Riderhood comes close to drowning once, before he finally goes under with Bradley Headstone. Eugene Wrayburn is rescued from a watery grave by Lizzie Hexam. Jenny Wren, Lizzie's friend, loses her grandfather to the river—an old man, dragged from the depths by Hexam, still wearing his nightshirt.

In the book, drowning and near drowning have a nearly cyclical rhythm that is echoed by events on dry land. A man goes under and vanishes forever or resurfaces as an unrecognizable body. The story the book tells is a movement *between* what is there and what is not there, a flux from the seen to the unseen. You can't have presence without absence, and language itself is born from this rhythm. The words can speak to what is missing. Where do words live if not in a zone between presence and absence?

This dilemma begins with the book's title, which is itself a nod to *between-ness*, an evasion of a proper name that would refer directly to the book's hero. This is not *Oliver Twist* or *David Copperfield*, in which the title introduces the hero. The title implies a relationship *between* or among people, points to a person defined through his connection with others. John Harmon is "our mutual friend," but you have to read the book to know that. Dickens's middle names were John Huffam, a fact that illuminates the author's stake in the book's mystery. He has buried his own *middle* names in his hero, whose pseudonymous adventure ends in rediscovering the name Harmon. To put it another way, even before you open the book to read it, you encounter a reference that is fundamentally obscure, because it points to nobody as of yet. Once inside the book, you find yourself confronted with more obscurity—the dim twilight, an incoherent form, dark water, dust flying through the streets—and before long you are swept up into a wilderness of unknowing at every level. Perhaps the problem of the novel is articulated best by one of its minor characters, Jenny Wren: "Misty, misty, misty. Can't make it out . . ."

The way into this foggy world is through metaphor. In Dickens, metaphor is *the* mode of perception. His books are veritable jungles of tropes, figures that became more and more unbridled as his abilities as a writer grew, and the careful reader must begin to unravel this dense metaphorical structure. It isn't easy. The entanglement of one trope with another is like a fast-growing vine that keeps sending shoots here and there, until separating its climbers becomes an awesome job. In *Our Mutual Friend*, tropes rarely appear as isolated moments of comparison that briefly yield new meaning. Instead, they linger and mark the narrative permanently, so that after a metaphorical event, the new meaning is adopted as if it were literal—the "vehicle" is changed forever. For example, early in the novel a servant in the Veneering household is compared to an "Analytical Chemist." From that moment on, he is simply "Analytical." The figure remains as a proper name, and the original simile is digested by the text. A roasted haunch of mutton served at a dinner party is compared to a vapor bath and the guests to bathers:

> And now the haunch of mutton vapour-bath, having received a gamey infusion, and a last few touches of sweets and coffee, was quite ready and the bathers came. . . . Bald bathers folded their arms and talked to Mr. Podsnap. . . . sleek whiskered bathers . . . lunged at Mrs. Podsnap and retreated; prowling bathers went about looking into ornamental boxes and bowls. . . . bathers of the gentler sex sat silently comparing ivory shoulders.

By the time the reader has reached the naked shoulders, the bath has been superseded by the bathers themselves. Early in the book, Mrs. Podsnap is compared to a rocking horse: "Quantity of bone, neck and nostrils like a rocking horse." Over a hundred pages later, she is seen in the act of "rocking." Metaphor is metamorphosis, and the changes are so swift that everywhere you look, people and things are shuddering as if the world won't sit still to be named.

Dickens also creates movement between the animate and the inanimate. The inanimate often looks human, and people often look like objects. When Fascination Fledgeby tries to gain entrance to a house, the reader is told that "he pulled the house's nose again and pulled and pulled . . . until a human nose appeared in the doorway." The metaphorical nose is followed by a literal nose, and the comic tension it creates undermines the status of both, making the "real" nose appear alien and disembodied, as if it were floating alone in the dark space of the doorway. The two "noses" are confused through similarity and proximity in a form of contagious magic—the stuff of animism. But Dickens's animism isn't truly magical. His nose doesn't disguise itself and run around St. Petersburg assuming dangerous social pretentions, as Gogol's does. It just hangs there. What does happen is that the seemingly stable boundaries between the man and the door are confounded. The ordinary world of houses and doors and door knockers and human bodies is not fixed. The lines of perception float.

Living in this world means instability, means being part of a shuddering dance of words that refuses easy definition. By tracing a single minor character, we can begin to understand how literal and metaphorical meanings play themselves out in the book and enfeeble conventional boundaries. From the descriptions of Silas Wegg, the reader is led through a maze of connections that find their way to the heart of the book's obsession with the body and its abstract associate: the self. Wegg, a shady street vendor, is often called just "the wooden gentleman." One of many characters in Dickens who has lost a limb, Wegg "seems to have taken to his wooden leg naturally." Silas suffers from what might be called creeping wood syndrome: the material of a dead limb is encroaching on his entire body, but this syndrome isn't limited to Wegg. He exists within a lavishly developed network of wood metaphors that *splinter* in all directions. Wood links him to the city in general, which the narrator calls a great "sawpit," blinding and choking its citizens, to "sawdust"—which links him to all dust—the over-whelming real and metaphorical presence in the novel. Dust mounds loom on the horizon—shapeless hills of valuable waste. Boffin, the "Golden Dustman," digs through dust mounds for objects not yet reduced to unintelligible particles. Silas Wegg seems to attract waste. The corner where he sells his wares is both chaotic and dirty: ". . . shelterless fragments of straw and paper got up revolving there, when the main street was peace; and the water cart as if it were drunk or short-sighted came blun-dering and jolting around it, making it muddy when all else was clean." Boffin's dead master, Harmon Senior, miser and dust mogul, made an empire from dust. Dust is good business, and it turns a profit, but it is still garbage, a fact which links Wegg to urban pollution in general, as well as to the corruption of the city's prominent "lords and gentlemen and honourable *boards*," who are accused of "dust shovelling" and "cinder raking" and producing a "mountain of pretentious failure." The route from Wegg to leg to wood to sawpit to dust to pollution, to paper, money, and city government is surprisingly direct. And each link in this metaphori-cal chain produces more associations, equally rich and simulta-neous, which find their way back to the human body and how to articulate it.

As it turns out, the wooden gentleman has stayed in touch with his amputated limb and goes calling on it. Walking through the door of Mr. Venus's gloomy shop of bones, Wegg inquires:

> 'And how have I been going on, this long time, Mr. Venus?'
> 'Very bad,' says Mr. Venus uncompromisingly.
> 'What am I still at home?' asks Wegg, with an air of surprise.
> 'Always at home.'

The "I" here is the bone, and Wegg's linguistic contortion is both hilarious and profound. To arrive at this "I," he must in fact *turn himself inside out* and adopt the third person as the first, but the comedy is also logical. At what point does the part cease to be I? Where is the threshold between the "I" and the "not-I"? Mr. Venus, who registers no surprise at Wegg's pronominal misuse, is an *articulator* of bones, a man who makes his living piecing together death waste. Therefore, it also comes as no surprise to the reader to discover that Mr. Venus has "dusty hair."

The absurdity of Wegg's wandering "I" returns when John Harmon tries to reconstruct the events that led up to his near death by drowning. This passage not only makes explicit the naming difficulty announced by Wegg but revives in new form the wood metaphors associated with Wegg, metaphors that have only an impoverished meaning when read in isolation. The comedy of Wegg's amputation becomes the image of an axe felling a tree and annihilation of the self:

> 'I was trodden upon and fallen over. I heard a noise of blows, and thought it was a woodcutter cutting down a tree. I could not have said that my name was John Harmon—I could not have thought it—I didn't know it—but when I heard the blows, I thought of the woodcutter and his axe, and had some dead idea that I was lying in a forest.'

Reading Wegg is like reading the novel in miniature—a plunge into a pool of language in which narrative and metaphor mingle and meaning accumulates until it overflows. As a model, Wegg's character suggests, first, that there is a relation between bodies going to pieces and the disintegration and pollution of

London in general, and, second, that this erosion, both corporeal and environmental, is somehow connected to dislocations in language.

2 The Framework of Society

Good order depends entirely on the correctness of language.

—Confucius

Naming people and things is fraught with difficulty in this novel. Dickens wills us back to the dawn of first questions, to what it means to call the world by name. Identification is Mr. Venus's business, and it's not a simple one. His murky shop brings to mind the novel's initial images of obscurity. Wegg looks into "the dark shop window" and sees only "a muddle of objects vaguely resembling pieces of leather and dry stick, but among which nothing is resolvable into anything distinct." Venus, however, is undaunted. "I've gone on improving myself," he says, "until both by sight and by name, I'm perfect." Dickens insists on the double meaning of *articulation* by making Mr. Venus an encyclopedist of the dead, a comic version of the Enlightenment man classifying decay. Wegg is given a verbal tour of the shop by its owner:

'A wice. Tools. Bones, warious. Skulls warious. Preserved Indian baby. African ditto . . . human warious. Cats. Articulated English baby. Dogs. Ducks. Glass eyes, warious. Mummied bird. Oh dear me that the general panoramic view.' Having so held and waved the candle as all these heterogeneous objects seemed to come forward obediently when they were named and then retire again.

It is Mr. Venus's voice that makes each object distinct, that calls forth individual objects from the muddle. Individuality comes out of the act of naming, not the other way around, and this ability makes Mr. Venus a creative figure in the book, acknowledged by Wegg as a man with a monumental task: ". . . you with the patience to fit together on wires the whole framework of society—I allude to the human skelinton." The "skelinton" is articulated bones. The bones of perception are articulated in words. Words are the "framework of society," but in this society, something dreadful has happened to them.

The word *society* refers to a particular group of characters in the novel, and this domain of the Podsnaps and their "bathing" guests, the fraudulent Lammles, and the Veneerings is given the full treatment of Dickens's crushing satire. When the Veneerings give a dinner party, the scene is described not directly but through its reflection in a mirror. Significantly, this long passage is written as a series of sentence fragments, each one beginning with the word *Reflects*. A single fragment gives the feeling:

> Reflects mature young lady; raven locks and complexion that lights up well when well powdered—as it is carrying on considerably in the captivation of mature young gentleman; with too much nose in his face, too much ginger in his whiskers, too much torso in his waistcoat, too much sparkle in his studs, his eyes, his buttons, his talk, and his teeth.

The use of the mirror damns society as flat, superficial, and illusory, but the reflection is also a field of brokenness, an image of piecemeal, not whole, bodies that returns the reader to Mr. Venus's bone shop. Like Dickens's joke of the two noses, the mirror subverts the conventions of body image. The dissection of the "mature young gentleman" makes no distinction between his garments and his body parts. There is no inside or outside, only a flat visual impression signaled in the refrain "too much," which applies equally to eyes and to buttons. The aged Lady Tippins, omnipresent at all of "society's" functions, is also hard to grasp as a whole being: "Whereabout in the bonnet and drapery announced by her name any fragment of the real woman may be concealed is perhaps known to her maid." There is inevitably something morbid about these descriptions of "society" and its creatures, a sense that these fragments smell of death. When Tippins rattles her fan, the noise is compared to the rattling of her bones, and when Eugene Wrayburn looks down at the ruined corpse of Radfoot early in the novel, he comments, "Not *much* worse than Lady Tippins."

Like many of her cohorts, Tippins is little more than a *name*. When Veneering decides to run for Parliament, he asks Twemlow, a meek little man, if his powerful cousin Lord Snigsworth "would give his name as a member of my committee. I don't go so far as to ask for his Lordship; I ask only for his name." In terms of the narrative, this is entirely reasonable. The name is what counts in society. The gentleman himself is quite dispensable. The cleft between words and the world resists closing. This is the story's metaphysical ache. Naming is arbitrary: signs appear to refer not to experience but to other signs.

While there is something noble about Mr. Venus's efforts to articulate bits and pieces of the dead, because his work is an attempt to make order from what is in the end hopelessly "warious," society resists meaning and order by allowing itself to be ruled by signs that have no referents. In *Our Mutual Friend* "the whole framework of

society" is disintegrating under the weight of its dominant sign—
money—which, not surprisingly, acts very much like dust:

> That mysterious paper currency which circulates in London
> when the wind blows, gyrates here and there and everywhere.
> Whence can it come? Whither can it go? It hangs on every bush,
> flutters in every tree, is caught flying by electric wires, haunts
> every enclosure, drinks at every pump, cowers at every grating,
> shudders upon every plot of grass, seeks rest in vain behind
> legions of iron rails. In Paris where nothing is wasted, costly and
> luxurious city though it be, but where wonderful human ants
> creep out of holes and pick up every scrap, there is no such
> thing. There it blows only dust.

As the dominant cultural fiction of developed societies, money
is an ideal nonsensical sign. Dickens penetrates the peculiar fact
that paper can be exchanged for something real, that money
serves as a society's founding gibberish, what Marx called "the
general confounding and compounding of all things—the world
upside down." But money is just one of a host of meaningless signs. One empty letter gives birth to the next. Veneering, for example, buys entrance to Parliament so that "he may
write a couple of initials after his name at the extremely cheap
rate of two thousand five hundred per letter." *L.S.D.* is exchanged
for *M.P.*:

> Why money should be so precious to an ass so dull as to
> exchange it for no other satisfaction, is strange; but there is no
> animal so sure to get laden with it, as the Ass who sees nothing
> written on the face of the earth, but the three dry letters L.S.D.,

not Luxury, Sensuality, Dissoluteness, which they so often stand
for, but the three dry letters.

Dry letters are everywhere. Dickens had a penchant for mysterious initials, acronyms, for alphabet jokes and pure nonsense. He
brings his reader close to the abstractness of signs, to the surprise
that these markings can be interpreted at all. As a young man, he
studied shorthand, and the account of his struggles with that new
alphabet is revealing. He called them "the most despotic characters I have ever known":

> The changes that were wrung upon dots which in such a posi-
> tion meant such a thing and in such another position meant
> something entirely different; the wonderful vagaries that were
> played by circles; the unaccountable consequences that resulted
> from marks like flies' legs, the tremendous effect of a curve in the
> wrong place, not only troubled my waking hours but reappeared
> before me in my sleep.

Dickens's use of the word *despotic* to describe the unintelligible characters is significant, because it suggests a hierarchy—the
reader laboring under the tyranny of signs. In *Our Mutual Friend*
there is a strong connection between despotic written characters
and paternal human characters. Fathers, real ones and figurative
ones, are the keepers of letters, member of a ruling class eager to
sire not children but paper. Veneering, for example, hosts the
"Fathers of the Scrip-church" and among them is "the father
of three hundred and seventy-five thousand pounds." Eugene
Wrayburn's overbearing father, who has pushed him into the law
but never actually appears in the book, is called simply M.R.F. (My

Respected Father) by his son. The ironic acronym stands in contrast to the meaning of the words, which are in effect devoured by the cryptogram. Twemlow, that modest participant in society's gatherings, has a father figure, too—Lord Snigsworth. He never enters the story in person, either. He appears only as a portrait hung on the wall. John Harmon's father, also invisible in death, is paper only, a figure who survives as nothing but text in the several conflicting wills he has left behind. These are paper men, mere ghostly markings somewhere between presence and absence. They are there, and they are not there.

Paternity, when associated with society, is usually mediated through signs or mirror images; and despite the fact that the thing these mediated forms represent is often unattainable, the paternal has power. Eugene stages several inner dialogues with M.R.F., and the paternal voice crushes the son with its blanket prohibitions. Harmon's ghost manipulates his heirs through his dust fortune. And other paternal figures, although they may appear bodily in the narrative, are similarly unapproachable. Podsnap never once addresses his daughter Georgiana by name. For her, he is a specular image. The narrator tells us that Miss Podsnap's "early views of life" were "principally derived from the reflections of it in her father's boots." Podsnap equates fatherhood with censorship. His job is to cut short conversations that he considers potentially injurious to "the young person": With "a flourish of his arm," he waves all undesirable subjects "from the face of the earth." And again the text brings us back to the dead body through a meaningless name. When Podsnap insists that the half dozen people who have recently starved to death in the streets of London are themselves to blame, Twemlow, the mild arbiter of good sense in the novel, objects. Podsnap accuses him of "Centralization":

He was not aware (the meek man submitted of himself) that he
was driving at any ization that he knew of. . . . But he was certainly more staggered by these terrible events than he was by
names, of howsoever many syllables.

Podsnap is the novel's supreme middle-class being, a man
ruled by repetition and summed up in the routine that signals his
character: "Getting up at eight, shaving close at quarter past,
breakfasting at nine, going to the City at ten, coming home at half
past five and dining at seven." The ritual allows for nothing but an
insular domestic rhythm. What happens in the "city" is not
included. The city where dust flies and people starve falls out of
the system. A reified language of resistance to the world, a language of exclusion and forgetfulness, Podsnappery resides in the
territory of the despotic signifier—of L.S.D. and M.P. and M.R.F.,
and of "ogolies" and "izations," systems that are meant to explain
experience. But the very idea of a system is that nothing is forgotten. Forgetfulness is the outlaw of system, and yet the language of
the fathers, the lawmakers, turns on repression and silence.

Paternity is a crisis of meaning in the novel, an alphabet soup
of nonsensical directives. Harmon Senior has left wills all over his
property, inheriting and disinheriting his son according to his lat-
est whim. Twemlow's powerful cousin, Lord Snigsworth,

puts him [Twemlow] under a kind of martial law; ordaining that
he should hang his hat on a particular peg, sit on a particular
chair, talk on a particular subject with particular people, and per-
form various exercises; such as sounding the praises of the
Family Varnish (not to say Pictures), and abstaining from the
choicest of the Family Wines unless expressly invited to partake.

The law of Snigsworthy Park is an absolute, arbitrary, military law erecting boundaries and thresholds that cannot be questioned: hang your hat here, sit here, say this. Paternal figures in the guise of military men appear several times in the book. Bella Wilfer dreams of a General husband, and Eugene explains that he chose M.R.F. because it sounds "military and rather like the Duke of Wellington." But the language of the despot is the blather of edict. Like Podsnappery, like last wills and testaments, *it does not and cannot tolerate a reply*. There is no rejoinder to this kind of speech, because even if an answer is given, it isn't heard. It is speech that annihilates the interlocutor.

If the law is by definition paternal—the site of symbolic separations through language—then Dickens presents us with a failure of that function. Symbolic structures appear as a muddle of blurred boundaries and meanings. But what is this all about? The failure is visited on the children. Denomination means being adopted into a community of speakers, and names are given by the father. Patronyms are signs of genealogy, legitimacy, and therefore coherence. They carry the weight of the past and a line of descendance. The father's name, borne by the legitimate and lost to the illegitimate, is the nexus for what becomes in Dickens a battle for a single name and a fixed identity. To have no legitimate name is to be no one. In *Our Mutual Friend*, Betty Higden explains to the Boffins that the love child she has informally adopted has "no right name." He is called "Sloppy," a name that unearths and repeats the novel's myriad metaphorical threads—sloppy, slop, garbage, waste, mud, fog, dust. Random coupling is a plague that destroys barriers and erases distinctions, for it creates a world in which children cannot identify their fathers, and therefore cannot identify themselves. But the issue of identity that shapes the stories of the novel cannot be posed as a simple polarity between a lawful name and an unlawful one; it is far more subtle than that.

Although John Harmon is legitimate, he suffers from the same fragmentation on the level of naming that Sloppy does. With typically ingenious metaphorical leaps, Dickens satirizes the law through the alphabet and then links its failure to the person of Harmon and his problems with his dead father. The law in the novel is exemplified in the droopy legal practice of Lightwood and Wrayburn. The young but already world-weary Eugene Wrayburn has gone into the law to please M.R.F., and his chief contribution to the office is not enthusiasm but a piece of furniture: a secretaire, described as "an abstruse set of mahogany pigeon holes, one for each letter of the alphabet." The lawyers, however, have few clients and the pigeonholes are empty. The alphabetical filing system refers to no real persons. It is the clerk, suitably named Blight, who invents clients for the firm when Boffin comes seeking legal advice from Lightwood and Wrayburn—"Mr. Aggs, Mr. Baggs, Mr. Caggs, Mr. Daggs . . ." But later in the story, the secretary comes up again when illiterate Boffin confuses this piece of furniture with the human Secretary, John Harmon, alias Rokesmith, who comes to ask for a job. "We have," he says, "always believed a Secretary to be a piece of furniture, mostly of mahogany." Within the world of the book, the mistake is a consistent one. Like the ghostly nobodies invented by the clerk for the law office, Harmon's pseudonymous existence is plural and arbitrary—a spectral existence indicated by the many names he is given in the book: Julius Handford, John Rokesmith, Secretary, Jack a Manory, Chokesmith, Artichoke, Sexton Rokesmith, Fortune Teller, Captain, Blue Beard, Mendicant, The Man from Somewhere, The Man from Nowhere, Ghost, and Nobody. Significantly, the missing name is the patronym: Harmon. In the pseudonym he keeps longest, Harmon holds on to his Christian name: John. The son's mock death becomes a way of circumventing the father's *will*, becoming invisible through a name change. What remains is a secretary, and whether furniture or human, it is a multiple anatomy of holes.

The mistrust of signs in *Our Mutual Friend* includes a mistrust of literacy itself. Wegg tries to teach Boffin to read, but the wooden gentleman's grasp of words is riddled by frequent mispronunciations and half-understood meanings. Lizzie Hexam accepts reading lessons from Eugene Wrayburn only after much thought, afraid not only of the seductive powers of her teacher but of the seduction of the signs themselves. Everyone who is normal acquires language. Not everybody learns to read. Reading is a further entrance into the abstraction of language and, in this novel, acquiring signs implies both distance and loss. But what does one lose? A critical connection to one's origin. For Lizzie Hexam's brother, Charley, literacy is a denial of his father and life on the river. He leaves home against his father's wishes and becomes the protégé of the schoolmaster, Bradley Headstone. The chapter in which Charley leaves home is called "Cut Adrift." The boy is disowned by his father, separated from his family, and refuses to heed his sister's warnings about remembering where he comes from. Education makes Charley blind—to his sister's goodness, to Headstone's treachery, and to his own selfishness. Charley learns to read signs, but he loses his past.

Gaffer Hexam is a unique father in the novel. He is the only paternal figure who cannot read. Even more than that, his attitude toward literacy borders on the phobic. He is also a *real* presence, not a reflection, ghost, or sign. The man has lovingly brought up his daughter, and this counts for a lot in a book populated by indifferent, cruel, or disconnected fathers. Hexam is identified closely with the river—the place of the drowned and the unrecognizable, of found corpses and refuse, the place where John Harmon forgets his name, a place where names disappear, where one thing mingles with another. It is liquid in the same way that maternal space is liquid—like being in the womb and the time of early infancy: a time before consciousness or when consciousness is just dawning, a time before language, or before language has properly taken hold of us, before words have beaten what is freefloating into a defined shape. Gaffer Hexam himself refers to the river's maternal function when he scolds his daughter for being squeamish about his "business" in the river. "How can you be so thankless to your best friend, Lizzie? The very fire that warmed you when you were a babby, was picked out of the river along side the coal barges. The very basket that you slept in, the tide washed ashore. The very rockers that I put it upon to make a cradle of it, I cut out of a piece of wood that drifted from one ship or another." The splintering wood of countless metaphors in the novel, from sawdust to the woodcutter in John Harmon's delirium, appears here as real wood dragged from the river. Gaffer recycles the river's debris to sustain life like a mother—warming, rocking, and caring for the infant. And that "best friend" is somewhere in the past, a debt to be remembered. If language is the ordering feature of our world and means immersion in the Symbolic Order, to use Jacques Lacan's term for it, it is clearly a gain, but it is also a loss. That early world is inaccessible except perhaps in isolated moments of unreason, not available to words. *Our Mutual Friend* is a book that in spite of itself wills the inclusion of the *unarticulated*, the forgotten, and the missing. Its language investigates the limits of language.

The novel creates a divide between *dry* letters—signs, symbols, literacy, which are associated with paternity, on the one side—and a *liquid* formlessness, on the other—the river, which is associated with the maternal. Characters caught between the divide face a double lure: a desire to drown themselves in oneness and a desire to back away in terror. But in the end, this simple division between two poles of human experience is not neat. It is troubled. The definition and clarity promised by the fathers usually don't arrive. Order and identity are supposed to issue from the very figures who are themselves immersed in filth and chaos.

3   Waste

The father is the one who punishes. Guilt attracts him as it does the court officials. There is much to indicate that the world of the fathers and the world of the officials are the same. . . . The similarity does not redound to this world's credit; it consists of dullness, decay and dirt. The father's uniform is stained all over; his underwear is dirty. Filth is the element of the officials.

—Walter Benjamin

Benjamin is writing about Kafka, but the passage applies equally well to Dickens. Despite their function as the keepers of law and order, many figures of paternal authority are subject to the obscuring properties of filth. Waste is the miser's domain in particular, and the book's particular miser is John Harmon's father, the king of refuse, who has so badly neglected his property that it, too, is turning to dust. It is helpful to remember that there were garbage brokers, or dustmen, in London during the nineteenth century and that Dickens is describing a real way of turning a profit in the city. Dust was shorthand for garbage, because of the immense quantities of ash that were discarded at that time. When the illiterate Boffin finds himself the garbage heir, he hires Wegg to read to him, among other things, Merryweather's *Lives and Anecdotes of Misers*. Among its tales is one about a Mr. Dancer, who lives in a house that has been reduced by neglect to a "heap of ruins." After he dies, "one of Mr. Dancer's richest excretoires was found to be a dung-heap in a cow-house; a sum but little short of two thousand five hundred pounds was found in this rich piece of manure." The parable makes money literally *indistinguishable* from feces. Freud made much of the connection between money and excrement, between holding back money and controlling one's bowels. In *Our Mutual Friend* coin and feces join together as the property of the "filthy rich." But there is something more to the story of Mr. Dancer. In order to uncover the treasure, the seeker had to bury himself in manure.

Waste is by definition that stuff we don't want. Waste from our own bodies is particularly important because it was *once us*, and by getting rid of it, we make sure it is *not us* anymore. Wegg's bone problem is essentially a question of symbolic borders and distances. When he says, "I should not like to find myself dispersed, a part of me here and a part of me there," he articulates a real human fear. The fact is our bodies are not closed but open. We breathe and eat and cry tears. We urinate and defecate, feed our children and enter each other sexually. The world comes into us and goes out of us. And when we die, *we are waste*. The rituals for the dead help us to draw a firm line between the living body and what it will inevitably become—a corpse. But what happens if those lines are not well drawn, if they wobble and begin to move, if we lose our grip on the symbolic boundaries that keep us from falling out of ourselves?

4   Madness

. . . the horror of the thing hideously behind . . .

—Henry James, *The Golden Bowl*

Bradley Headstone goes mad. In him the failure of symbolic definition becomes psychosis, and the schoolteacher suffers from a loss of self in doubling, delirium, and seizures. Dickens does not give us Headstone's personal history, and this blank is significant. All we know is that, like Charley Hexam, the schoolteacher has cut himself off from his past. There are no parents or siblings in his story, and their absence speaks to his utter isolation. Dickens gives a portrait of an unintegrated personality that goes to pieces under the strain of an overpowering libidinous desire.

The narrative presents Headstone's psychic turmoil in terms of signs, their failure, and the disintegration that follows. In his classroom, the schoolmaster is the embodiment of the dry and empty letters that crop up everywhere in the novel. As master to children, Headstone plays a paternal role, and like other fatherly figures, his relation to signs is one that does not bother with meaning:

> . . . the exponent drawling on to My dear Childererr, let us say,
> for example, about the beautiful coming to the Sepulchre; the
> repeating of the word Sepulchre (commonly used among infants)
> five hundred times. And never once hinting what it meant.

In this passage the word *sepulchre* resonates as a kind of double tomb: for the pupils its meaning is absolutely vacant, while for the reader it signifies the container of a corpse. But the word also refers to the "exponent," Headstone, whose name means a *marker* for the dead, a *name* above ground. What you don't see are the fragments of flesh and bone that lie underground. Headstone's relation to language reiterates the narrative's alarm about that which cannot be articulated—a fissure between the name on the surface and the mess below. His language, in the form of repetitive lessons in the schoolroom, provides a form through which he can indulge in the unspeakable—the reenactment of his brutal attempted murder of Eugene. Like a headstone, the words conceal a ruined body:

> . . . as he heard his classes he was always doing it again and improving on its manner, at prayers, in his mental arithmetic, all through his questioning, all through the day.

This zone behind or beneath words in Headstone is given the startlingly apt name "T'Otherest." It is Rogue Riderhood who gives Headstone the nickname, derived from his perception of three men he links in his mind: Lightwood, whom he calls "The Governor"; Wrayburn, whom he calls "T'Other Governor"; and Headstone, who is "T'Otherest Governor" and then simply "T'Otherest." The three designations are like successive images in a multiple mirror, terms descriptive of the increasing instability that marks the three men. But "T'Otherest" is also a sign of internal shifting in the character of Headstone. When Headstone disguises himself as Riderhood, to carry out his planned murder of Wrayburn, we are told that the clothes of his double suit him better than his own. He moves between one persona and another, between schoolmaster and T'Otherest, shucking off his identity as master to become like Riderhood, the *Waterman*, and is eventually sucked into the river, where identities vanish.

Headstone is a character who literally cannot *contain* the forces inside him: "The state of the man was murderous and he knew it. More, he irritated it with a kind of perverse pleasure akin to that which a man has in irritating a wound upon his body." The schoolmaster's sadism is also masochism—torturer and tortured occupy the same psychic ground. The battle tears him apart. He can't control his movements. When he speaks to Lizzie, his face "works" horribly. The spasmodic movement of his hand is compared to "flinging his heart's blood down before her in drops on the pavement stones." He pounds a tombstone in the graveyard and his knuckles bleed. He suffers nosebleeds, too, that come from nowhere, and then from seizures, sudden epileptic fits. He says to Lizzie, "I have no government of myself when you are near me or in my thoughts." The bleeding, the seizures, the words that rush from him are linked as expressions of violated boundaries, volcanic eruptions from unknown depths. His confession of rage and turmoil, hopelessly inappropriate, pours from him like a running wound. The fits affect his body as if there were no controlling consciousness; each part flies into involuntary movement. And when it is over, he cannot remember what has happened to him.

The metaphorical pulse of the novel quickens when Headstone is present. The images of ruin and filth that proliferate in relation to the novel's landscape assume force as metaphors of pyschic reality. The inner states of delirium and unconsciousness mirror the outer conditions of fog and filth that obscure the body. Of Eugene, Headstone says, "He crushed me down in the dirt of his contempt." As he nears death, his face turns pale, "as if it were being overspread with ashes." Headstone loses the edges of himself, and his speech disintegrates. The narrator tells us that he has increasing difficulty *"in articulating his words."* He stammers and chokes, his words are enunciated in a "half suffocated" voice. To

Lizzie he confesses: "It is another of my miseries that I cannot speak of you without stumbling at every syllable, unless I let the check go altogether and run mad." These are lapses of otherness, of a monster that finds no category except the monstrous. Like Wegg's bone, T'Otherest cannot be articulated into a comprehensible form.

5   I *and* It

"This world," Riderhood says, and "T'Other world." The relation between the living and the dead is a frame for the novel as a whole, and the word *other* comes to designate the tug-of-war between the two. Otherness in Headstone and in the narrative as a whole does not signify what passes between one subject and another, between *I* and *you*, but what passes between *I* and what once was *I* but is now *it*. There is nothing clean about the separation between what is alive and what is dead in *Our Mutual Friend*, and the lack of a hygienic cut is seen in the novel's play with pronouns. How do you refer to a corpse? Mr. Inspector, the policeman called in to investigate Gaffer Hexam's death, gives his version of the man's demise: "He sees an object that's in his way of business floating. He makes ready to secure that object. . . . His object drifts up, before he is quite ready for it. . . . he falls overboard. . . . The object he expected in tow floats by, and his own boat tows him dead." But the Inspector addresses the "object" he is bringing in as "you" and then further complicates matters by announcing over the corpse, "I still call it *him*, you see."

The Inspector's pronominal difficulty reverberates with Wegg's wandering *I. You* has become *it*, but perhaps not completely so, and may still deserve to be called *him*. Wegg's confusion of subject and object, which both animates his dead limb and dislocates the *I* as the sign of human consciousness, effectively dismantles the *I/you* axis of discourse, or what Emile Benveniste calls "the polarity of person," by confusing it with "non-person" *he, she,* or *it.* Benveniste writes,

> There are utterances in discourse that escape the condition of person in spite of their individual nature, that is, they refer not to themselves but to an "objective situation." This is the domain we call the "third person." The heart of the difference between person and non-person is seen in the fact that the polarity of person is reversible—I can always become you, and you, I, while this is not true of non-person—she, he, and it.

But all pronouns are shifters, and they have a fragility that nouns don't have, a greater motion and flexibility that Dickens readily seizes upon in the book. When learning language, children acquire pronouns last of all words, and aphasics lose them first. Schizophrenics may confuse *I* and *you*, as if the difference between them can't be grasped. *I* is not a simple designation but a complex one. It is where we all live inside language. Losing it means losing ourselves.

Jenny Wren's alcoholic father cannot say the word *I*. Robbed of his paternal function by his own drunkenness, he is infantalized by his daughter, who calls him "bad boy" and "wicked child." Mr. Dolls is a walking area of devastation, consistently referred to by the narrator as "it" rather than "he":

> The whole indecorous, threadbare ruin, from the broken shoes to the prematurely grey scanty hair, grovelled. The very breathing of the figure was contemptible as it laboured and rattled in that operation like a blundering clock.

Mr. Dolls is given his name by Eugene Wrayburn, because Jenny Wren is the "doll's dressmaker." But the name points to him as a person who is *like a thing*, and Mr. Dolls either refers to himself in the third person or drops the *I* altogether: "Poor shattered individual. Trouble nobody long," he says, but the muttered phrase he repeats over and over in his defense is: "Circumstances over which had no control." These are the same circumstances under which Harmon is supposed to have died: "and that the said John Harmon had come by his death under highly suspicious circumstances" and also, "He [Harmon] had lapsed into the condition in which he found himself, as many a man lapses into many a condition, without perceiving the accumulative power of its separate circumstances." The word *circumstances* acts as a synonym for *otherness* in the novel—that inchoate zone of the third person that rises up to disfigure, erase, and silence. A man has trouble speaking. He begins to stutter and loses control of language—the very stuff that makes him human. He loses himself. Without an *I*, there can be no *you*.

Dialogue is possible only with *mutual* recognition. When Bradley Headstone cries out, "*I* have been set aside and *I* have been cast out," he has reached the end of reciprocal speech. Wrayburn insults Headstone by referring to him as "Schoolmaster," not by his name. "I don't know why you address me—" Headstone says, and Eugene snaps back, "Then I won't." The humiliation annihilates. I do not address you. You do not exist. Self-consciousness is born in another person. It grows from that essential relation and can't exist without it. Dickens's story of recognition is Hegelian, dialectical. We are all made through the eyes of another, the place where we are recognized and called by name. As John Harmon says, "A spirit that once was a man, could hardly feel stranger or lonelier going unrecognized among mankind than I feel."

Later, an unrecognized man who was once John Harmon tries to piece together the mystery of his own narrative, the circumstances of his own "death," but his memory is spotty. Here is the passage in full:

'Now, I pass to sick and deranged impressions; they are so strong, that I rely upon them; but there are spaces between them that I know nothing about, and they are not pervaded by any idea of time.

'I had drunk some coffee, when to my sense of sight he [Radfoot] began to swell immensely. . . . We had a struggle near the door. . . . I dropped down. Lying helpless on the ground, I was turned over by a foot. . . . I saw a figure like myself lying on a bed. What might have been, for anything I knew, a silence of days, weeks, months, years, was broken by a violent wrestling of men all over the room. The figure like myself was assailed and my valise was in its hand. I was trodden upon and fallen over. I heard a noise of blows, and thought it was a woodcutter cutting down a tree. I could not have said that my name was John Harmon—I could not have thought it—I didn't know it—but when I heard the blows, I thought of the woodcutter and his axe, and had some dead idea that I was lying in a forest.

'This is still correct? Still correct, with the exception that I cannot possibly express it to myself without using the word I. But it was not I. There was no such thing as I, within my knowledge.

'It was only after a downward slide through something like a tube, and then a great noise and a sparkling and crackling as of fires, that the consciousness came upon me, "This is John Harmon drowning! John Harmon, struggle for your life. John Harmon, call on heaven and save yourself!" I think I cried it out aloud in great agony, and then a heavy, horrid, unintelligible something vanished, and it was I who was struggling there alone in the water!'

This remarkable monologue encapsulates the novel as a whole. Harmon's return to life comes with the memory of his proper name at the very moment he recognizes himself from outside himself—as a person who has been named, as someone who is part of a community of speakers and therefore part of the world. And this event of regaining the self is imagined as taking place after the violence of a birth or rebirth, complete with a bizarre slide *"through something like a tube."* After he emerges from the tube, he finds the name and sees himself. Before the drowning, he is doubled in Radfoot. Only when he calls himself by name does he reclaim the double as himself. This time, the double as mirror image serves as a therapeutic vision of the self as whole. Harmon's telling is an agonizing re-collection of the broken, unrecognized body that lies at the heart of the novel. This alienating moment of seeing one's self—of doubling and reflection—is a moment of crisis that results in either cohesion or distintegration. John Harmon, Bella Wilfer, and Eugene Wrayburn are rehabilitated through others and find a place within the community. Bradley Headstone, Riderhood, and Mr. Dolls go to pieces. By pronouncing his own name, Harmon expels the *it*, the "heavy, horrid, unintelligible something"—the abject corpse of the other man—which is also his own drowning, his own death, and his own corpse. Then and only then is it possible for Harmon to find himself inside language and to use the word *I*.

6   The Dream of a Common Language

When one does not possess the categories of recollection and repetition
the whole of life is resolved into void and empty noise.

—Kierkegaard, *Repetition*

From recognition and singular naming comes an image of wholeness—the fully articulated body and the *I*. Those characters who have stable names, who are not beset with myriad nicknames and pseudonyms, display a power to revive and heal that is not given to characters with multiple appellations. Lizzie Hexam, for example, is only called Lizzie. The purity of Lizzie's name throughout the novel contrasts starkly with the fickle Bella Wilfer, who is riddled by many designations. Lizzie watches the fire and sees images of "fancy" in it, while Bella looks in her mirror at a reflection she calls, among other things, "Beast" and "Dragon"— further images of the monstrous, unknowable self. But Lizzie is the one who hauls Eugene from the river, a body so badly disfigured that, the reader is told, his own mother might not have recognized him. When he hovers between life and death, the *word Lizzie* becomes a vehicle of rescue for Eugene: "The one word Lizzie, he muttered millions of times." The repetitions are agitated, fitful. He utters the name in "a hurried and impatient manner with the misery of a machine" and then "in a tone of subdued horror." Eugene's palilalia recalls both Headstone's teaching and the mechanical sputterings of Mr. Dolls, and like these pathological repetitions, it is a symptom of a fall into that borderland between life and death, the very place where John Harmon loses and then finds himself. Indeed, the narrator calls Eugene's feverish utterances "the frequent rising of a drowning man from the deep." When Lizzie touches him, the palilalia stops. In a moment of lucidity, he says to her, "When you see me wandering away from this refuge that I have so ill deserved, speak to me by my name, and I think I shall come back." Again and again, Lizzie recalls him from insentience. Hers is a purely human magic, which gives language the confidence of creation—of calling something—someone—into being. The critical distinction between demonic and magical utterance lies in the difference between speaking to no one and speaking to someone.

The name *Lizzie* is a bridge between death and life. But *Lizzie* is also an incantation on the road to a word Eugene has been unable to speak. Jenny Wren gives Mortimer Lightwood the word to say to Eugene:

> He stooped, and she whispered in his ear. She whispered in his ear one short word of a single syllable. Lightwood started, and looked at her.
>
> 'Try it,' said the little creature, with an excited and exultant face . . .
>
> Some two hours afterwards, Mortimer Lightwood saw his [Eugene's] consciousness come back, and instantly, but very tranquilly bent over him.
>
> 'Don't speak, Eugene. Do no more than look at me, and listen to me. You follow what I say.'
>
> He moved his head in assent.
>
> 'I am going from the point where we broke off. Is the word we should have come to—is it—Wife?'
>
> 'O God bless you, Mortimer.'

The potential sentimentality of this passage is undercut by its oddness. Dickens frames the entire scene around a word—which he points out is "of a single syllable." The word *wife* is passed on from one speaker to another as a *translation* or *transformation* of *Lizzie* into its collective context, the proper name changed into a signifier of a social role. *Wife* refers to a relation between people. It is the claiming of an identity that is formed through another and in the presence of others, and in this way it is like the novel's title—a designation that may be claimed by many through others. Eugene cannot arrive at the word by himself. *It must be given to him,* and this single word begins the process of his rebirth. In this moment, among these people, language is being reclaimed as a structure of meanings that brings definition to human relations.

Lizzie's power is rooted in memory. She is able to rescue Eugene, because she has learned the skill from her father and has not forgotten how to haul a body from the depths. The novel's primary mnemonists are all women, and all women whose names are not subject to change. They are also characters conspicuously *not* prone to drowning. Drowning and its metaphorical associates— doubling, going to pieces, scattering into plural identities—are all part of the book's driving fear: the fear of the corpse or of the unintegrated, formless body, which is identified with maternal space through the river. But these female, often maternal characters are not threatening representatives of the chaotic space. On the contrary, they tame the wilderness through imaginative memory. Betty Higden, for example, who is a kind of lower-class saint, pulls together what is left of her family, ripped apart by poverty and death. She is subject to mild fits or visions that she calls the "deadness." "There's a deadness steals over me at times. . . . Now I seem to have Johnny in my arms—now, his mother—now his mother's mother—now, I seem to be a child myself, a lying once again in the arms of my own mother. . . ." The word *dead*, associated with corpses, filth, and disintegration throughout the novel, is regenerated here through a vision of coherence that links the past and the present in the single physical act of holding and being held. Similarly, Mrs. Boffin, surrogate mother to the Harmon children when they were small, is haunted by faces that appear before her in "Harmony Jail"—the name given to Harmon Senior's decrepit mansion:

> 'The faces of the old man are all over the house tonight. . . . For a moment it was the old man's, and then it got younger. For a moment it was both the children's and then it got older. For a moment it was a strange face, and then it was all the faces.'

Both Betty Higden and Mrs. Boffin bind together in space what has flown apart in time: a family. Haunted by visions of resemblances, Mrs. Boffin, the only mother John Harmon has ever known, fills in the identity of the strange face as the lost son and, in doing so, brings the *unrecognized* spirit back from the dead. Betty Higden's and Mrs. Boffin's visions stand in opposition to the disintegrating surfaces of mirrors in the book, because they are pictures of relations among families that bring together the dead and the living. This rhythm of generations is part of a natural cycle of giving birth, growing old, and dying, and herein lies the healing impulse of the novel. What these women imagine is essentially what Mikhail Bakhtin describes as "idyllic time," the time of folklore, which connects human life to the literal ground of experience. Time and space come together through countless generations who have shared the same earth. Bakhtin opposes "idyllic time" to "biographical time," which is the temporal sequence of an individual life cut off from nature and so from regenerative possibility. But Dickens's use of idyllic time is not purely folkloric. It is not the earth that binds one generation to another but the articulation of that common ground through a common language.

When Harmon recalls the event of his near death, his speech is an attempt to gather the fragments of the past into a semblance of coherence, into a narrative. His memory is pervaded with gaps that disturb time, disturb story, gaps that are metaphorically bound to Mr. Venus's incompletely articulated bodies. The "French Gentleman," at first only a ribcage, gains a few more parts here and there as the story progresses, growing like a tiny model of narrative. When utterance becomes story, the coherence of narrative can fight the corrosion of forgetting. And a tale always presumes a listener, even if the one who hears is within the self. Dickens portrays the task of recollection as wrenching labor. The holes in Harmon's narrative remain unfilled, but the telling, with its insistence on accuracy ("Is this still correct?"), is a struggle to articulate cryptic pieces into a whole as Harmon plays detective, investigating his own near death. The narrative must pass over "spaces" and "silences"—spots of absence and forgetfulness. It is impossible not to read the events Harmon recounts as an inner battle. Its only characters are a number of faceless men, "a figure like myself," an "unintelligible something," and a teller who denies the validity of using the word *I* to tell his tale. Like Oedipus, Harmon is both subject and object of his investigation, a search that at every turn unveils a version of the self.

"I find myself an embodied conundrum," says Eugene Wrayburn and "Riddle-me-ree." Headstone suffers a seizure and forgets. Harmon cannot remember. "My mystery," he says. Memories are pieces of the self—the mysterious jumble of the past in the present—and the novel's central act of reconstruction, which comes to mean going home, making a narrative circle that takes the hero or heroine back to his or her origin. John Harmon must travel back before he can begin again. Memory must be movement, supplying the effective concatenation between one moment of life and the next. It must be repetition, but repetition with difference.

Jenny Wren, who supplies the magic word *wife* to Lightwood, is another feminine visionary in the novel. With the scraps and refuse from Fledgeby's corrupt business she dresses her dolls, each one filled with the novel's primary stuff: sawdust. Unlike Mr. Venus, who uses waste to articulate dead bodies, Jenny uses it to form new, imaginary bodies, lilliputian beings she manipulates to tell stories. And unlike Betty Higden's and Mrs. Boffin's visions, what Jenny sees are transcendent fictions. Her strange hallucinations of radiant children dressed in white, and of beautiful birds and flowers, are drawn from the stuff of story and myth: "I smell the white and the pink May in the hedges and all sorts of flowers that I was never among." From the rooftop she calls to Riah:

> The call or song began to sound in his ears again, and looking above, he saw the face of the little creature looking down out of a glory of her long bright radiant hair, and musically repeating to him, like a vision, Come up and be dead! Come up and be dead!

Like Betty Higden's "deadness," Jenny Wren's call reverses the spatial scheme of dying in the novel, in which bodies disintegrate underground or sink into invisibility in the river. The strange song also reverses the emptiness of the chanted word *sepulchre* in Headstone's classroom. Her repetition is a call for resurrection, a movement up to air and sky, with which Jenny identifies herself through her name *Wren*.

But Jenny Wren has named herself. Her real patronym is

Cleaver, a word which, through its allusion to cutting, summons the countless metaphors for fragmentation that sweep through the novel. And *Cleaver* remains a haunting subtextual presence in *Wren*, because along with her rapturous visions, the doll's dressmaker delights in sadistic fantasies, dreaming of the day when she can torture her imaginary future husband, whom she refers to only with the pronoun *Him*. She will pour burning liquid "down his throat . . . and blister it and choke him." *Cleaver* is Jenny's "T'Otherest"—the part of her that was born into a paternal vacuum and the part of her that is crippled. She cannot walk without a crutch. The difference between Headstone and Wren is not a difference between real sadism and fantasy (Jenny fulfills a torturous wish by putting pepper on the plasters she uses to bandage Fledgeby) but a difference between incomprehensible and meaningful signs, of replacing dry letters with meaningful ones. Indeed, when Headstone and Jenny meet, their encounter is figured through a sign. The schoolmaster lies, and one of Jenny's creatures, Mrs. T. for Mrs. Truth, hides her head in shame. The letter *T* in *Mrs. T* marks the only time in the novel that a letter or initial is used to signify full meaning. Jenny, like her creator, is an artist, and in *Our Mutual Friend*, art is in the business not only of restoration but of reincarnation through narrative: the stuff of truth.

The secret of Jenny's art is that it employs a common language. The children of her hallucinations resemble popular Victorian representations of angels, and the birds and flowers are taken from pastoral conventions. By transfiguring people from her life into the stock characters from fairy tales, she orders a chaotic world into a secure narrative scheme. Riah is her "fairy godmother" or "the Wolf," depending on what she sees; Fledgeby is "the Fox" or "Little Eyes." Her use of fairy tale is also a bid for idyllic repetition, a way to counter past losses. She asks Riah to "change Is into Was and Was into Is." Her desire to tamper with time, to turn the present into the past and the past into the present, is part of the novel's idyllic movement toward the time of folklore and fairy tale. "Once upon a time . . ." is no time, and it is in this unspecified time, with minor qualification, that Dickens chose to set his novel: "In these times of ours, though concerning the exact year there is no need to be precise. . . ." Jenny Wren asks her friend for the magic of narrative itself, which turns the written past into the present time of reading.

Many tales are alluded to in *Our Mutual Friend*, but none more often than "Little Red Riding Hood." The name *Riderhood* collapses the story's title into a single name through which the waterman becomes devouring wolf, a role that strikes at the very heart of the novel's dread: a child is deceived, eaten up, and then freed by a passing huntsman, who cuts open the beast and frees the grandmother and the child from the wolf's belly—an image that mimics birth. The perfect story about the fear of engulfment and disappearance, about the loss of identity in something boundless and monstrous, "Little Red Riding Hood" reenacts Harmon's story of drowning and rebirth. The paternal cut of the huntsman's knife restores boundaries, breaks inside from outside, and resurrects the heroine.

The story is a frightening one, but the form of the telling is itself a weapon against fear, and in this novel, the chief artist and storyteller is a little girl. Fairy tales, like Dickens's own books, are stories about children; the youngest of three sons or three daughters—often the child who is thought to be stupid and has been sadly neglected at home—sets out on a journey. Many of Dickens's children are real or emotional orphans, and the paths they take must eventually lead them home. But in *Our Mutual Friend*, home is not real. You cannot really go back, after all. Time has passed. Home is a fiction, an idyllic landscape of the mind—a language, not a place—through which otherness, chaos, and absence are tamed by stories that reinstate the true law.

And so, near the end of the book, we find Lizzie and Jenny quietly reading on the rooftop. Beyond the roof's edge, smoke billows and dust flies, but the girls have made themselves a meager garden from a few "humble flowers and evergreens." When Fledgeby arrives and tells them that "not much good" will come of such literary efforts, Jenny snaps back at him, "Depends upon the person." This sensible retort answers the other, debased readers in the book. Neither the act of reading nor signs are in themselves evil. Double meanings, ideological rhetoric, nonsense, pathological repetitions, and cryptic codes make language dangerous, simply because these words cannot be understood. Jenny and Lizzie are readers, and their book lies at the heart of an idyllic garden of common words, as does Dickens's own.

And we find Bella telling her father stories by the river. The place of disappearances is rehabilitated through her projections of the voyages she imagines upon it. In these stories, Bella mends her father. Her stories turn the weak, browbeaten, childlike "Pa," known by innumerable names, among them "R.W.," "Rumpty," and "Cherub," into a figure of respect and power:

> Now, Pa in the character of owner of a lumbering square-sailed collier, was tacking away to New Castle, to fetch black diamonds to make his fortune with; now Pa was going to China in that handsome three masted-ship . . . to bring home silks and shawls without end for the decoration of the charming daughter. Now John Harmon's disastrous fate was all a dream, and he had come home and found the lovely woman just the article for him . . . and they were going away on a trip in their gallant bark . . .

[with] Pa established in the great cabin. Now John Harmon was consigned to his grave again, and a merchant of immense wealth (name unknown) had courted the lovely woman, and he was so enormously rich that everything you saw upon the river sailing belonged to him.

Like Scheherazade, Bella tells one story after another, a series of seductions that postpone ending. One voyage becomes another and another while the blank of the husband's name remains unfilled. Bella's temporary resurrection of John Harmon echoes Dickens's own narrative play with Harmon's life and death and with his name and namelessness. Only at the very end of the novel is the gap filled permanently with the name *Harmon*, the name that Bella will share. Even Jenny Wren's *HE*, that pronominal blank associated with her negligent father, gains a proper name—Sloppy, and it is to Sloppy that she acknowledges Riah as her "second father," substituting the protective and kind friend for the shattered infant father. Lizzie Hexam, whose love for Eugene is bound up with her love for her dead father, depicts her desire as an opening—"Only put me in that empty place, only try how little I mind myself, only prove what a world of things I will do and bear for you." And Harmon says of Bella, "I will go into a blank life, leaving her." Desire is that empty place that propels the story forward, that moves toward an ending in which absence is filled.

Closing these gaps is an act of the imagination. The rooftop garden is not beautiful, but the readers there imagine that it is. Rumpty doesn't change. He is refashioned by Bella's stories. Eugene tells Mortimer of his love for Lizzie: "The glow that shone upon him as he spoke the words, irradiated his features so that he looked for the time, as though he had never been mutilated." Eugene *is* mutilated. His speech seems to counteract disfigurement, because it is lodged in real dialogue with another person, and it uses the magic words of love.

I am made through your eyes. Because of you, I can imagine myself as whole. I remember some things. I forget others, but when I tell you my life, I give it the shape of a story and that story is myself. Without it, I am nobody. This is not a Cartesian view of human identity. The self in *Our Mutual Friend* is not a given. It discovers its singularity through others and then within the structure of language itself, which is both inside us and outside us. Our very selves are articulated from these common words. But language is not identical to the world, and in all of us there live the muffled forms of what came before words. Every once in a while, those forms return in the delirium of a fever or in a dream, in a fear we cannot explain, or when we look on the dead. Those are the moments when we lose ourselves. Finding ourselves again is a trick of "fancy," as Dickens calls it, a mutual understanding of the stories we share.

Ghosts at the Table

Traditional still life is easy to recognize. It is the painting of things. The objects are usually small and most often set out on a table. The things are not outdoors but inside a house, and the represented space is not deep but shallow, which makes the spectator feel close to them. Still life does not include people. It implies human presence but doesn't show the living human form. Painting the inanimate world is different from painting people or nature, for the simple reason that paintings, like things, are *still*. Landscapes may depict storms at sea or a gentle breeze blowing across a meadow, but the paint is motionless. Portraits may imply the movement of a hand, the beginning of a smile, but the human beings on the canvas are stopped in that instant forever. Like all mimetic painting, traditional still life is in the business of illusion. Only a mad person would reach out to take a grape from a Chardin canvas in order to eat it, and yet the fact is that the painting of a table laid for dinner, flat as it is, bears a resemblance to the reality of the things it refers to by virtue of its deadness. The

French *nature morte* bears this aspect of still life in its name. The genre as a whole exists within the human relation to things— essentially a relation between what is living and what is dead.

The idea of things and only things as a suitable subject for painting dates back to antiquity; since then, the genre has labored under the weight of its insignificance. Painting a pear or a dish was never as important as painting a person. The still life has always been lowest on the rung of art's hierarchy. The depicted subject was crucial in determining the significance of the work of art. Nevertheless, things have always played a role in art, and the problem at hand is to sort out the differences. A Byzantine icon may contain an object, but the depicted thing was not meant to look real. It was filled with the magic of otherness—the rendering of the sacred was itself sacred. And even with the growing humanism of the Renaissance, things in paintings carried symbolic and mythical value. It is the Dutch who are credited with the rise of still life, who moved the detail of a canvas to its center and made it a full-fledged genre; but even then, no matter how mimetic the images, ethical and religious ideas inhabited the objects seen in the painting. The very marginality of still life would make it attractive to modern artists and give it a subversive edge. They could play with the old hierarchies but refuse to give in to them.

And yet the rise of the humble object as a suitable subject for painting cannot be separated from the sense that the ordinary might hold a viewer's interest—that a simple thing could be charged with power. It is true that without the striving, growing merchant class and its accumulation of material wealth in seventeeth-century Holland, the sparkling glasses, dishes, pipes, fruits, meats, and animal carcasses could not have been elevated to the status of a painting's sole subject. The still life embodied a new emphasis on the significance of the everyday. And this vision of the pedestrian as something interesting, as something worthy of interest, has never left the genre.

When I was in Chicago last summer, I went to the Art Institute, and among the paintings I saw was Chardin's last work. It is the picture of a table with a simple white cloth. On the table is a sausage, bread, a glass, a knife. It is an image so simple, so without drama, that it is difficult to describe its effect. When I looked at the painting, I was overwhelmed by its pathos. My eyes filled with tears, as if I were looking at a scene of a dying child and not at a table with sausage on it. I cannot fully explain this emotion, but reading Diderot, I discovered that he felt something similar about Chardin: "This magic," he writes, "is beyond comprehension." Norman Bryson, in his fine book *Looking at the Overlooked* (Harvard University Press, 1990), notes that Chardin avoided arrangements that looked arranged and that the blurring of paint near his frames allows the spectator an illusory entrance into the room. Chardin creates an intimate, familiar domestic space that has a strong relation to human gestures. But more than this, his painting evokes for me what is not there. The man or woman who ate of them is no longer at the table; but the food, the utensil, the glass are still charged by that unseen human presence. And because the missing person cannot be reduced to a particular sex, to a unique face and body, the spectator who peers into the space and the one who has left it share the table more completely. The fact is I do not imagine the absent people as painted images but as living beings.

In Jerusalem, I had a similar experience, at the Israel Museum, with real things. Found with the Dead Sea Scrolls were a few objects: among them, a basket and a plate. The basket, mostly intact, was identical to one you could buy today in any market in the Mediterranean. The plate was of pale green glass with a simple geometric design around its edge. It could have been made yesterday. Two thousand years stood between me and those objects, and yet in their familiarity and constancy, time vanished. A nameless woman used the plate the way I use my plates. She carried food in her basket the way I carry groceries in mine. Were I to come face-to-face with her by some enchantment, the cultural distances between us would be vast, but through these objects we are linked. It is Chardin's simplest still lifes—the late ones—like *Glass of Water with Coffeepot* that stir me most deeply. Like the basket and plate behind glass in the museum, Chardin's paintings make me feel reverence for what it means to be human. We breathe. We eat. Then one day we die.

Our eyes continually roam over the world of things, and we notice things more when we are alone. A human face will always draw our attention away from objects; but in solitude, objects are the company we keep. Chardin's canvas is as silent and the things he represents in it are as motionless as they are in life. But the canvas itself is also a thing, an object that, like many objects, outlasts human beings, and its survival is written into the idea of the painting itself. Real bread goes stale, real sausage decays. The table, the glass, the utensils, however, might remain intact for generations. But we are not looking at bread or sausage or wood or metal, but paint, as Magritte's famous pipe joke would later openly announce. We are peeking into a framed space of illusion, but it is an illusion Chardin makes convincingly. Chardin's still lifes are not allegorical, as were the Dutch and Flemish painters'. Their grand theme of Vanitas becomes in Chardin the simple truth of mortality. We are all ghosts at Chardin's table.

A hundred years before Chardin, Juan Sanchez Cotan painted still lifes that inhabit a radically different universe. His luminous

fruits and vegetables have an uncanny clarity that jolts the spectator. It is not a problem of recognition. I recognize each food in
Quince, Cabbage, Melon and Cucumber, and yet these fruits and
vegetables do not remind me of those in my own kitchen, as
Chardin's do. It is as if these foods have been overexposed. The
melon reveals a surgical slash made by a knife's incision. The sus-
pended cabbage and quince, the resting melon and cucumber are
immaculate, discrete entities. The painting's effect relies on the
clean separation of one thing from another. In this work, no food
touches the other. As Bryson points out, Cotan's still lifes are
rooted in the monastic life he lived as a lay brother of the Car-
thusian order, an order that emphasized solitude. Bryson links
Cotan's painting to the imaginative use of the senses in Saint
Ignatius of Loyola's Spiritual Exercises. In Cotan's work, vision is
heightened and sharpened.

When I look at this food, I am awed, and I would guess this is
exactly the feeling I am supposed to have. In the world, food
becomes part of the body. It enters us, is used, and the excess is
expelled as waste. Digestion blurs the line between the eater and
the eaten. In Chardin, there is a comfortable relation between the
absent bodies and the food that is meant to enter them. In Cotan,
we know we are looking at food, and we know that food is to be
eaten. In this painting, part of the melon has been consumed, but
eating is part of a larger order of things, an order that relies on
clear separations—among them, a clean cut between the body
and the outside world. The fasting and sexual abstinence prac-
ticed by the Carthusians as acts of purification and denial are
attempts to seal off the body from the outside. This is not an
impulse limited to religious orders. Modern anorexics are driven
by a similar desire. Bryson evokes the Spiritual Exercises to illuminate the role of vision in approaching the sacred, but the Exercises

also present us with a formal schedule of classification and discipline, by which means daily life may be perfectly ordered. In his book *Sade, Fourier, Loyola* (Hill and Wang, 1978), Roland Barthes notes that the Exercises propose a way to completely cover the day, so that no moment is free. This absolute coverage takes pictorial form in these precisely rendered and neatly distinguished fruits and vegetables. (I can't help thinking of the seven-year-old who has a horror of his peas sliding into his mashed potatoes.) Behind the food is a black, rectangular void. This dark space is not the space of perception. It is unreal, abstract, and it suggests not a solid wall but infinity. This is food as sacred gift shining inside, not a human order but one ordained by God. When I look at this painting, I do not feel the presence of the brother who ate that piece of melon. I do not even feel the painter. I am alone, staring into something both strange and incomprehensible. Like a monk, I am alone with God.

Chardin and Cotan may be said to occupy the psychological poles of still life. Chardin eases every separation, between the viewer and what is viewed but also among the objects he paints. There is no strain in looking at his food and objects. It is their very ordinariness that enchants them. Cotan is all strain, discipline, and withholding, qualities so rigorous that the ordinary becomes extraordinary.

Most of Dutch still life painting resides somewhere between these two poles. Willem Claesz's painting *Vanitas* serves as a good example of a middle ground. In it we see smoking paraphernalia, a plate, knife, bowl of fruit, a strangely tilted glass vase, and a skull. It is a somber image. The silver bowl is opulent and beautiful but dimly illuminated; a subtle gleam of light appears on its base, a gleam echoed on the vase, which then reappears more dimly on the skull. Without the skull, the painting would be different, but it would remain sobering. The objects on the table are not in perfect order, but the scene isn't slovenly either. It is true that the plate hangs slightly over the table's edge, as does one of the pipes, but it isn't in danger of falling. The object that does seem precarious is the vase, tipped dangerously to the right. The object's angle seems to imply that it is about to shatter. As I look at it, the tension between the left and the right side of the canvas begins to seem dramatic. My eye is pulled from the upright form of the bowl over to the leaning vase and tipped skull. It is a movement from relative order to disorder, which is then restabilized by the vertical candleholder above the skull. This is not an image of chaos but one in which order and chaos, life and death coexist and define each other. Of course, Claesz's skull carries the message of universal mortality far more pointedly than Chardin. The skull is the ultimate meeting ground of the spectator and the object, because we are projected into it. *I* will eventually become *it*. The skull, along with animal carcasses, is a recurring image in still life. These things qualify literally as still life, as *nature morte*, because, in death, living creatures become objects. The depiction of a human corpse would share this quality, but showing whole human bodies, living or dead, is not traditionally part of the genre. The skull, however, fits neatly on a table. It is important to note that a human thighbone could never have the power of a skull. The skull retains the outlines of the human face, and people are drawn to it. This attraction is very possibly a physiological one. Infants are drawn to faces almost immediately. The holes in a skull, in which there once were eyes, the empty cranium, which once was the seat of an individual consciousness, carry the clear traces of a living past.

The skull returns again and again in the form. Max Beckmann's 1945 *Still Life with Three Skulls* uses the old image to new and terrifying effect. Claesz is reminding us of mortality. Beckmann's table with skulls, a bottle, and playing cards reminds us of recent human slaughter. Soutine's *Carcass of Beef* (1924) is similar in its intent. This canvas vividly shows us an animal's bloody entrails and with it the suggestion that the animal has just been killed. The longer you look at it, the more you feel that its screaming ended only moments ago. In all of these still lifes, from Cotan to Chardin to Claesz to the modern examples of Beckmann and Soutine, the canvases are drenched with meaning. They cannot be reduced to "messages." The great allegorical paintings of the Dutch are not one-liners. The relationship between an object and the way it figures in these allegories is neither simple nor direct. Chardin's still lifes are heavy with emotion, but the production of that feeling cannot be reduced to the depiction of one object or another. Nevertheless, these works draw from and play with a known pictorial vocabulary through which they produce complex meanings.

Cézanne wanted something different. His still lifes are phenomenological. The spectator is alone and supreme, and the appetite that remains is one for looking, not eating. I am not tempted by Cézanne's pears in *Still Life with Ginger Jar and Eggplants*, because they are not pears. They are forms in the space of my perception (just as the ginger jar next to them is). The pears are elevated, not out of their thingness but out of their ordinary role as food. And the light has changed. Chardin, like the Dutch and Flemish before him, worked within the darkness of thick walls and filtered light, but now the doors and windows have been thrown open and light shines onto these objects to illuminate them as *prelinguistic* entities. It may seem odd to speak of images in terms of language. Pictures are supposed to escape the confines of words. But language is the grid through which we see the world, and in still life, naming is implied in looking. The humility of the depicted things creates a more direct relation between the noun and its meaning, a relation that is less direct, for example, in a narrative history painting. The food and vessels of Chardin are all named and known. They live inside a universe of fully articulated domestic habit that comforts us with their familiarity. There is a clove of garlic sitting next to a coffeepot. It has rolled toward the edge of the table, probably during the preparation of a meal. In Cotan, the identification of each fruit and vegetable designated in the title is cast in an almost terrifying clarity that seems to enhance its identity as God given, as though the painter is striving toward a pre-Babel world. The wonder of Cézanne comes from refusing the categories of a given, common language. What Chardin celebrates, Cézanne rejects.

His still lifes feel both undomestic and unfeminine. The food and objects he paints have been drained of their household functions, their semantic content. His objects appear *denatured* by the act of looking itself. Most people have experienced the odd sensation of estrangement that comes from looking long enough at a single object. For all of us there was a time before we knew what things were called, and then the world looked different. Cézanne's still lifes are a rigorous effort to return to a vision unburdened by meaning. In a letter to a young poet in 1896, in which he complains about his growing fame, he writes, ". . . were it not that I am passionately fond of the contours of my own country, I should not be here."[1] The word *contours* is revealing. He does not say *landscape*. He says *contours*. Cézanne was searching for contours that would make us see again, in paint, what we have lost to language. The flatness or distortion of his canvases, the things that sometimes appear to float on the canvas, serve this alienation. It is as if these objects cannot be fully assimilated into their names. A part of them flees the word and lives in its contours.

In some way the project Cézanne set for himself is impossible. Because we can identify the things he paints, they cannot be stripped of meaning, and yet within this idea of seeing the world anew is also the proposition that paint is the medium in which to do it. Cézanne does not hide the existence of the brush but lets the strokes show, and by flattening his perspective, he tacitly acknowledges the canvas as a canvas. But Cézanne is not joking or teasing his viewer with some notion of art for art's sake. The project on view in Cézanne's still lifes and the sensuality of these objects is serious. Cézanne said again and again that he was interested in looking at nature, and he had a passion for discovery that was never completely satisfied. After all, light and air never rest. Cézanne painted the same place and the same things over and over again, in a constant search for the real through the imaginary. These still lifes show us mutability, not because we know that pears in the world rot but because these pears appear to exist within a larger continuum of nature that is in constant flux.

Cézanne, as is universally acknowledged, left a deep imprint on modern still life. Matisse's still lifes bear the lessons of Cézanne. He, too, democratizes the visual field—flattening foreground and background into one, encouraging the spectator to take in one thing as much as another. But Matisse's things are not denatured. In *Still Life with Blue Tablecloth*, I say to myself, There is a beautiful blue tablecloth with a coffeepot, a bowl of apples, and a green bottle illuminated by sunlight shining into the house. The coffeepot retains its connection to domestic life without this fact being particularly important. When I look at these still lifes by Matisse, I remember that ordinary things at home are also beautiful—a white pitcher on my red table, yellow roses in a blue vase. But looking at Matisse is not like looking at things at home. It is more like a vivid, very recent memory—the imprint that remains after you have closed your eyes to the image in the light.

Cubism adopts Cézanne's idea of a new look at things without his devotion to the idea of unearthing an idea of the real—whatever the cubists may have claimed. Cubist still life canvases are lively, intellectual exercises that dissect ordinary vision in the interest of perceptual play. Their strength is in bringing an almost musical rhythm to the genre, so that the classical Dutch convention of showing instruments in still life becomes an evocation of music's real movement, not only the idea of music as one of the fleeting pleasures we may indulge in before we die. And yet no matter how surprising these canvases must have seemed at the time, they are unmysterious. They articulate objects as much as Chardin does, but without the larger sense that this articulation is a pact of human fellowship. In cubism, even if the image is blasted to bits, a guitar is a guitar is a guitar, as long as we can detect its strings. Recognition is investigated but not subverted, as it is in Cézanne. Forceful, fun, and overtly masculine, cubism quotes the still life genre for its own purposes.

Classical still life has continued to thrive in the twentieth century. Giorgio Morandi's miraculous bottles fall within the tabletop genre and tantalize the viewer with a strange dynamic between belief and doubt. His bottles suggest at once their identity as bottles in the world and an existence as spectral as Platonic shadows. If you look long enough at his paintings, the forms seem to change in their light—not sunlight but light from some imaginary source. As in Cotán, we cannot approach these images without awe. They reside in a space of otherness that may still be construed as a table.

Picasso, Klee, and Magritte all worked squarely inside the genre at times, but unlike Morandi, they did not find a home there. Philip Guston is the most recent artist I can think of whose use of still life was not a conservative nod to an old genre but a revolutionary gesture. In his late works, Guston does not refer back to a classic form but reinvents it. His drawings in particular—of shoes, books, brushes, pencils, ladders, cans, bottles, cigarettes, trash can lids, and nails—are unlike earlier still life and utterly different from the blank images of pop art that preceded his late work. Guston said himself that he was over-whelmed by a desire to draw objects, that he felt "relief and a strong need to cope with tangible things."[2] Still life in Guston seems to happen as part of a larger project that also includes the human figure and that bears a powerful relation to the body. An untitled drawing with a hand and a cigarette smoked backward (1967) feels to me very much like still life, except that, in this case, what is implied in Chardin—the gestures of a body—is included, not excluded. The gesture is also inverted, creating a comic complication unallowable in Chardin. The presence of a hand in Chardin's work would disrupt its stillness. Here the hand seems to be another object in the world of objects. And while the things Chardin paints remind us of a universal domesticity, Gus-ton's pictures are personal images of a particular inner life that begin to gain resonance for all of us.

His images repeat themselves in a mobile creation of new meanings. It is as if he is in the business of inventing a new syntax of the banal. The shoe, for example, turns up again and again. The drawing of an untied boot from 1967 is infused with a sense of comic sadness, while *The Door* (1976), in which we see a crowd of boot and shoe soles almost entirely blocking an open door, com-municates alarm and sexual discomfort. But the shoe is a labile entity, a true poetic form. In the remarkable *Painter's Forms* (1972), a man's profile with an opened mouth appears to spew forth, among other things, a cork, a boot, a sole, and a bottle. An infant's first experience of the world is through its mouth, when it takes milk from its mother. For the first few years of life, in fact, the mouth is the primary organ of discovery. As all parents know, small children stick every object they can get their hands on into their mouths. But the mouth is also the place of speech, and *Painter's Forms* is an image not of devouring but of expelling a vocabulary for painting.

In *Painting, Smoking, Eating* (1973), Guston links three human activities, the latter two of which are undeniably oral. And because all lists give equal status to the noun inside it, painting is associated with smoking and eating. There is no hand visible in this picture. A man lies under the covers in bed, a cigarette stuffed in his invisible mouth. Beside him are the materials of his art. Again we see shoe soles. But we are unable to tell whether these soles, some heavily outlined, some dimmer, are representations of footwear or the footwear itself. It does not matter. What we witness is not a man actively painting but the stillness of a head and its wakeful dreaming. This smoking head allows things to come into it, consciously or unconsciously, willy-nilly. The boots that fill that doorway remind me of nothing so much as my own semisleep dreams in which forms keep changing and then sometimes fix themselves into an unsettling picture dredged up from a secret place in my own psyche.

In Guston there is a rare harmony between the poetic texts he often used in his drawings and the images near them, despite the fact that the drawings are never straightforward illustrations of the words. The poems of William Corbett and Clark Coolidge, for example, are inscribed into the drawing without disjunction. Guston wrote out the texts himself with his own hand. The drawings and the words are both gestural. *Painter's Forms* is exactly what it says it is. Objects, Guston seems to tell us, are my new medium. Through them I articulate myself and the world in which I live. They are not limiting forms but liberating ones. They are outside me and inside me. They are of my body and not of it. Guston's still lifes speak to the fact that the world penetrates us. We eat, smoke, and have sex. But language and images enter us, too. They become us. And in art they are spewed forth again, transfigured and renewed.

Still life is the art of the small thing, an art of holding on to the bits and pieces of our lives. Some of these things we glimpse in the frame of a painting are ephemeral—food, cut flowers, tobacco—and others, like the clutter in a dead man's attic, are objects that will survive us. The paintings speak to our wish to live and to our dread of dying, but because the space inside the frame is a figment and the things it holds are imaginary, they have the eerie quality of the impossible: a permanent dream. I often dream of objects, and when I do, they are always close to my nose. I am pressed up against them—a toothbrush or a pair of scissors or a pen. They are dreams of uncanny scrutiny. Dreaming is part of living, and its images are a form of memory in which the stuff of the everyday is recycled. Art is a kind of memory, too. A sausage is reinvented on a canvas. I will never cut it or eat it. But it is there in a parallel space that I enter nevertheless, and even though Chardin's painting is no longer in front of my eyes, the image remains. It has fixed itself in my mind as no real sausage ever could. Still life, like all art, happens through selection. One thing is chosen over another, and through the artist's choice, my eyes find a new focus. Chardin's painting is not a reflection of the tables laid with sausages and knives that I have seen in my own life but a spectral reincarnation of that familiarity. The experience of looking at art, like the experience of dreaming, is often more concentrated than waking life. Despite the inimitable present tense of every painting, it is always about the past. I do not mean its duration—how many years the canvas may have hung on a wall. I mean that what I am looking at is the representation of a thing which has a history in the mind and body of another person. I am looking at a work—at a "painter's forms." And this looking is a little like having someone else's dream. Because the objects of still life are ordinary—a sausage, a melon, a bowl, a boot—their translation into paint intensifies them. They are dignified by the metamorphosis we call art.

NOTES

1. Quoted in *Cézanne* by John Rewald (New York: Abrams, 1986), p. 221.

2. Quoted in *Night Studio: A Memoir of Philip Guston* by Musa Mayer (New York: Knopf, 1988), p. 141.